Dalit Literature & Minority Discourse
India and America

Dalit Literature
&
Minority Discourse
India and America

Edited by

Suman Bala
Deepmala Sengar

Prestige Books International
New Delhi

Published by
Prestige Books International
New Delhi 110 060
prestigebooks@gmail.com
Phone: 9818755529

Associate Office
11B, Broomwood Road
London SW11 6HU

Associate Office
P.O. Box 2250
Sydney 2001

ISBN: 978-81-943009-1-5

Printed in India

Contents

Minority Discourse

The Americas

Book Reviews

Emergence of Minority Discourse: Dalit Writing in India and America

SUMAN BALA
DEEPMALA SENGAR

Dalit or subaltern designates the lower social classes, social groups relegated to the margins of society. Literature pertaining to these classes is often labelled as dalit or subaltern studies. In India, Dalit relates to the backward or suppressed people since ages, and in the West it denotes writings on or by blacks and the history of their sufferings at the hands of the white population.

Dalit literature being a revolutionary form of literature often does not adhere to the traditional principles of aesthetics. Dalit writers, by and large, derive their inspiration from B.R. Ambedkar who surely is the cult figure in the field of Dalit literature and politics. The Ambedkarite consciousness reflects a dalit identity and calls for justice, freedom and equality in society.

Dalit literature is akin to African American literature, produced in the United States by the writers of African descent. To begin with, African American literature was dominated by autobiographical spiritual narratives. In her brilliant study of colonial culture across the globe entitled *Crippled Minds: An Exploration into Colonial Culture*, Sri Lankan scholar Susantha Goonatilake argues: "Colonial culture arises from the imposition of a European-derived culture on those areas of Asia, Africa and the Americas that has dominated over the last five centuries" (Vikas, New Delhi, 1982). An examination of various cultures of these regions reflects how the Eurocentric culture made impact on these and story of their survival whatsoever.

Responses to colonial culture have varied often showcasing the split between the original culture the immigrants belonged to and the place of their adoption. In the case of Africa, where the earlier traditions were non-literate and not an outcome of a strong urban culture, responses of a strong rejection of the colonial society and complete rejection of identification with it, are quite evident. African literature of the blacks, even at the non-cultural level, was vehemently rejected, and even abused by the Europeans.

The sense of estrangement and rejection that the sensitive black felt in the whiteman's homeland while trying to adapt to the latter's conventions is evident in the following poem:

> I feel ridiculous
> in their shoes
> in their evening suits
> in their starched shorts
> in their hard collars
> in their monocles
> in their bowler hats.
>
> (L. Damas "La Complainte du Negre" *Pigments*, Paris, 1963, 39)

The poet, in these lines, reacts to the alienation felt and establishes an intense identity with the primitive life and culture. There arose a constant question in their mind of "Who and what are we?" They found no logical reason to accept it: it was the blacks' odyssey to awaken and rebel against the hostile surroundings.

In the last few decades, African Americans' status in American society has immensely changed. There is now much greater focus on the writings of black writers. The present volume has some significant articles on both dalit writing in India and black writing in the U.S.

II

Minority Discourse provides a platform for the surfacing of the voice of the suppressed classes and it is to be understood as part of a revolutionary praxis in the interest of social change. The emergence of minority discourse is tantamount to making effort on the part of the minorities to herald their irrevocable presence. The present volume aims to offer minority discourses associated with a more dominant cultural tradition of the west. As a matter of fact, dalits or minorities are in many ways the subjects of social practices and should be treated as social agents, in much the same way as majorities. It is argued that minorities require specific protections to ensure that they are not marginalized.

III

Again like India, America has a number of minorities. In sociology, a minority group refers to a category of people who experience relative disadvantage as compared to members of the dominant group. Minority groups often face discrimination in multiple areas of social life, and this is no less true of minority literature. A case in point is the diasporic writings by Indians in the U.S.

For several years now, Indians have been going to the U.S. in search of jobs, fortune and better opportunities. They lagged behind in the nineteen seventies and eighties as they were busy consolidating their lives and working on economic security. They have now emerged as the most prosperous and highly educated community with family values. As the community grew, they became more prosperous and developed confidence and indulged in other activities—literary, cultural and political. Though still on the margins, they have embraced the Western life balancing it with Indian culture and heritage. Their writings embody a rich minority discourse that has energized and enriched the corpus of American studies.

The literature of the Indian diaspora in America has gained significant ground and is the burgeoning field of postcolonial literature in English. Salman Rushdie, Rohinton Mistry, Bharati Mukherjee, Amitav Ghosh, Vikram Seth, Jhumpa Lahiri, M.G. Vassanji and Shauna Singh Baldwin have attained international recognition. Though their writing constitutes yet a part of the minority discourse, they have forcefully challenged the tenets of the mainstream literature. While the early generation of immigrants from India constantly nursed their grievances against the country of their adoption, the current generation takes pride in their accomplishments and no more feels estranged, thus turning 'diaspora experience' into the 'mainstream' flow.

IV

Another area of investigation, which may be treated as subaltern or minority discourse, is that of folk literature. How come that Folk Studies has been relegated to the background in the recent times? The folk is said to owe its birth in the universal desire to listen to stories. "Tell me a story," the child demands, especially when he goes to bed. Very often, mothers and grandmothers tell stories when pestered by children. These stories, seemingly simple and funny, conveyed their understanding of the world, their ideas and beliefs, their customs and festivals, and even about birds and animals.

It is amazing that though the same stories are repeated over the centuries, they do not lose their charm. The secret is in the satisfaction that our basic curiosity finds in the folktales. Listening to them, we marvel at the mysteries of the world and especially many inexplicable phenomena of universe around us. Through the folktales, we seem to be widening our horizon of life.

There have been a number of folktale collections popular in Europe during the middle ages which indicate their source point to India: *The Fables of Bidpai*, *The Seven Wise Masters* and

Barlaam and Josaphat. Joseph Jacobs, as early as 1912, made an in-depth study in this area and concluded that "a goodly number of the fables that pass under the name of Samian slave Aesop were derived from India", especially from Jatakas and Birth-Stories of Buddha. Besides Joseph Jacobs, there are a number of British scholars like Miss Freve, Miss Stokes, Mr. Campbell who published folktales in such periodicals as *The Indian Antiquary* and *The Orientalist*. All these scholars traced the origin of the folktales to India.

It is a pity that the present generation of grannies, especially in towns and cities, are not so well conversant with traditional folk. The reason for this decline is more socio-economic than cultural. They are so engrossed in day-to-day matters of existence that they do not find enough time to relate the tales. Villages in India, however, have not undergone a drastic change. The inhabitants are still simple in an environment which has not changed much. This is in contrast to the people living in countryside in the West, who have adopted modern ways of life.

In the olden times, the supreme allegiance of Indians was not only to political rulers, but also to their country and the Nation, which embodied their spiritual-cultural values and aspirations. There was an intrinsic relationship between people and the surroundings. Ecology is therefore clearly linked with folklore of the nation. It is especially true of the areas in the valleys and mountains, lakes and rivers, trees and bushes. Inhabitants of these areas have a deep reverence for nature and mythologize it in their writings. "The formidable aspects of Nature," says Usha Bande in her illuminating book *Folk Traditions and Ecology*, "which the early man could not comprehend was responsible for the folk beliefs in animal and spirit worship, ghosts and demons, and other supernatural forces.

In the West, folk literature has been identified more often with America. The exaggeration and extravagance of American humour is said to have derived from the ingredients of folktales.

The comic element is the hallmark of most of the American folktales. Many of the adept and artistic writers transformed meanings and subtle messages into mainstream folk literature.

There are a number of folktales popular in the United States today—"A Baker's Dozen," "Bear Lake Monster," "Adventure on the Rogue" and "Hoop Snakes." In Canada, we have "Crow Brings the Daylight" and "Blood Knife." Folk music has contributed significantly to the social and aesthetic culture of America. Many of the songs reflect the struggle, empowerment and perseverance of the African American community, thus embodying the struggle of marginalized people in America. Folk music is therefore important from the historical point of view as it offers a lively picture of Africans marching ahead in their fight for civil rights.

American folklore encompasses the folk traditions that have evolved on the North American continent since Europeans arrived there in the 16th century. Native American cultures are rich and diverse; they explain myths and legends that explain natural phenomenon—like how the earth was formed and where humans and other beings come from. Before the advent of printing machine, people were telling stories, reciting poetry and singing songs about their beliefs, dreams and experiences. Much of the material that formed part of American folk literature was passed by word of mouth from generation to generation.

While folk has been frequently used by American writers overall, it is in fact writers of African descent who have often resorted to folk myths and beliefs in their writings. The Harlem Renaissance from 1920 to 1940 was a period of the flowering of African American literature, notable writers being Langston Hughes and Zora Neale Hurston. The Harlem Renaissance marked a turning point in the history of African American literature as it is then that these writings came to be absorbed into American culture. Within a short time, it ignited interest in African folk and culture.

Zora Neale Hurston is the best known name in the area of black American folklore. She was a scholar of anthropology. She has therefore been regarded as one who sharpened her penetrating insights into the value and strengths of culture and its roots. With a great zeal and enthusiasm, she highlighted in her work "African presence" in African American fiction.

It is to be noted that folklore and Black Cultural Consciousness are closely knit. This is so because Black people share their past history to a much greater extent than do other Americans. As a result, it is their history, rather folklore, which has helped them to survive and sustain their culture.

Since Hurston was an anthropologist as well as a novelist, she could imbibe qualities of both the areas and blend them into her writings. This is equally true of Indian American novelist Amitav Ghosh who being an anthropologist could use his knowledge of the human history and geography to weave it in the body of his novels. Anthropology has given vast knowledge and analytic tools to produce quality fiction to both the novelists.

Hurston is a black feminist whose work has ushered in a new period of female characters, reflecting the image of a 'new woman.' She is in many respects a literary forerunner to Toni Morrison and Alice Walker. In the recent years, her work has drawn a great interest in India, especially in the way she has blended folklore with feminism resolutely and inextricably.

Hurston made a deep research seeking information regarding Voodoo rituals which she has mentioned in her books of folklore: *Mules and Men* and *Tell my Horse*. Her works throw a significant light on Voodooism: it is a religion of creation and life. It is primarily the worship of the sun, the water and other elements of nature. No wonder, Hurston has become a metaphor for the black women writers' search for tradition. Most of writers like Alice Walker, Gloria Naylor and Toni Morrison sought inspiration from Hurston for the spiritual kinship interest in such relations and the mystery of the world. It is admirable the way

Hurston's works reflect a unique amalgam of folklore and fiction. She sketched characters in her novels who are undeniably human; they serve as beacon lights for all those who 'ain't ne'er de light at all," says Alice Walker.

It is pertinent here to point out that African American culture shares many of its characteristics with that of aborigines in Australia and Maoris in New Zealand. Indigenous people in Australia are commonly known as the Aborigines. They descended from groups that existed in Australia and surrounding islands before the British colonization. It may be noted that in common parlance, the term "black" has often been used to refer to indigenous Australians since the British settlement. While originally related to skin colour, the term indicates the aboriginal heritage or culture and refers to any such people, regardless of their level of skin pigmentation.

The Maori and Metis in New Zealand are indigenous people who arrived there in several canoe voyages between 1250 and 1300. Over several centuries in isolation, the settlers developed a unique culture, with their own language and mythology. Traditional Maori culture has undergone a significant revival in the recent decades.

This is true of similar people in America, Canada and New Zealand. Primitive people in all these countries believe in a number of practices and ceremonies based on indigenous and oral traditions. They have great reverence for the land and other elements of Native. Aborigines, as also Africans, had developed unique instruments and folk styles. This subsequently led to the emergence of Jazz dance and music, and also branched into rock and roll, hip hop and reggae.

Folktales reveal a marvellous wealth of knowledge and wisdom the indigenous people had, much contrary to the perception held by some modern thinkers. In an article "How ignorant we are of indigenous wisdom?" (*Asian Age*, 9 August 2019), Francis Gonsalves draws our attention to this aspect: "down-to-earth wisdom of indigenous peoples." This is amply evident in some of the folktales of India as also of other courtiers. Many of the present-day scholars dub indigenous peoples 'primitive', judged within the framework of science and technology. But many of the concepts and ideas contained in the folktales teach us valuable lessons, says Francis Gonsalves in our relationship with (a) mother earth (b) the Divine Being and (c) the life-in-community. The folktales are replete with the ideas and philosophy of the olden people—their love and reverence for the elements of nature, especially about our attitude to mother earth. Our overzealousness has led us to destroy nature's most valuable gift—forests. This has demeaned our life and living. Adivasis regarded the divine-human-cosmos as one seamless entity with which the ecologists the world over seem to agree. This intuitive approach has captivated and whetted man's love and appeal for the folktales which carry a rich wisdom and open up avenues for modern man.

V

Over to the Americas now: Colombia, Canada and the U.S.A. We need to highlight the contribution of these countries to world literature The Americas constitute a major segment of the earth's population: they comprise mostly the continents of North and South America. It has more than a billion inhabitants, two-thirds of which reside in the U.S., Brazil or Mexico. Various languages are spoken in the Americas. Most popular language of Anglo-America is English, though Spanish is the official language in some of these countries. French, along with English, is the official language of Canada.

Latin American literature is essentially the literature of the region Latin America; it is written in several languages, viz., Spanish, Portuguese and the indigenous languages of the Americas. It gained prominence globally in the second half of the 20th century, with the international success of the style known as 'magic realism.' This pushed Latin American literature onto the world stage.

Gabriel Garcia Marquez is a Colombian novelist, affectionately called Gabo throughout Latin America. He is one of the best writers in Spanish language. In 1967, he published his masterpiece *One Hundred Years of Solitude* which sold a record thirty million copies. The novel earned him the coveted Nobel Prize in 1972. After writing this novel, Marquez returned to Europe, to live in Barcelona, Spain, for seven years. Due to his outspoken views on U.S. imperialism, he was denied visa to enter the U.S. When Bill Clinton was elected the U.S. president, he lifted the ban as he confessed that *One Hundred Years of Solitude* was his favourite novel.

Erich Maria Remarque, the German-born American author is best known for his novel *All Quiet on the Western Front* which described the utter cruelty of the war from the perspective of a twenty-year-old soldier. The novel is a landmark in the vast-expanding literary horizons in the Americas.

The fiction of Elias Khoury is a rich minority discourse. Khoury is a Lebanese writer and an eminent intellectual. He has published ten novels in Arabic which have been translated into several languages. He was involved in the establishment of the Democratic Left Movement in Lebanon, founded in September 2004.

African American and Indian Dalit: Twins of Tragic Legacy in Two Continents

HEMANTH M.
NCWEB, University of Delhi

> We hold these truths to be self-evident, that all men are created equal, that they are endowed by their Creator with certain unalienable Rights, that among these are Life, Liberty and the pursuit of Happiness.
>
> "The US Declaration of Independence"

As is the case of race in USA, the superstructure of caste problematizes the selfhood of the subaltern in his relationship with the institutions of society such as family, church, school etc. It was Antonio Gramsci who defined 'subaltern' as one who lacks both freedom and voice in front of hegemonic superstructures of society which on the other hand conditions him to believe in the ethos and principles of the dominant. Gayatri Spivak in her famous essay "Can Subaltern Speak" uses the term 'subaltern' in the same way as Gramsci did and talks about the plight of subaltern women who suffer double victimization due to their economic and political powerlessness. According to her, it is the duty of modern intellectuals to ensure the representation of subaltern women voice while reviving the experiences of the marginalized. Hence, it is necessary to consider both Black and Dalit feminist writings as expressions of subaltern women voice in their attempt to ensure their representation in these respective literary traditions of the marginalized. Alice Walker's concept of 'Womanism' has initiated a wave of Black women's writing in the literary landscape of America through challenging the ethos and dogmas of African American male narration. In her famous essay "In Search of Our Mothers' Gardens," Walker defines "womanist" as "a Black feminist or feminist of colour" (xi). Moreover, she attributes a heroic stature to the Afro-American women, thereby giving them a voice of recognition in the male centric African American literary tradition.

Walker's decision to claim an independent space for Afro-American women writing has been further strengthened by Toni Morrison who through her literary masterpieces created a silent revolution in the world literary landscape. As Henry Louis Gates, Jr. puts it, "This tradition within a tradition is often related to, yet independent of the Black male tradition and its triangle of influence, Richard Wright, James Baldwin and Ralph Ellison" (*Reading Black* 2). Though Walker's *The Color Purple* and Morrison's *Beloved* have been studied extensively, it was mainly not a cross-cultural approach but with the tag of American context. In spite of the significant structural differences that segregate the genres of novel and autobiography, the purpose of this paper is to creatively excavate the social, political and cultural parallels between Dalit feminism and African American womanism through the analysis of authors from these respective literary traditions in order to develop a cross-cultural perspective.

Unlike the self-centric narration of male writers such as Douglass or Limbale, the distinct selfhood of both Black women characters in these novels and Dalit women writers in their autobiographies are rooted in the philosophy of commune, which gives them the necessary mental potential to survive during physical and psychological trauma. This harmonious blending of collective identity with that of personal makes these both writings identical. Whether it is Sethe in *Beloved* inspired by the life-story of slave Margaret Garner or the unfortunate Celie in *The Color Purple*, their self as is depicted in the novel is never individual but collective. Their existence itself is rooted in the feeling of commune manifested itself in forms such as family, church, friendship etc. and its solidarity, sometimes in its internal conflict. Their vigour to fight for physical and emotional survival in the midst of chronic tyranny and brutality derives from the strength of community feeling. Similar collective identification of marginalized self is vividly evident in the life-narratives of Bama and Kamble which further emphasizes the testimonial qualities of these distinct literary proclamations. While replying to the question of collective identity in her autobiography, Bama said, "How can I think of my life as one individual's? I am a Dalit and a woman . . . therefore it is my community which makes me what I am . . . my story is my community's story" (Mangai 116). Similarly, Baby Kamble in the beginning of her life-narrative *The Prison We Broke* declares her inseparable bonding with the commune when she writes: "I always loved being with my grandparents, that is my aai's parents. They belonged to Veergaon, a village in the Purander taluka in Pune district. The village was small and so was the maharwada. But the people in the maharwada were large-hearted. They were poor, of course, but they were very affectionate and simple, ready to even lay down their lives for someone they loved." (1)

If male writers of both Black and Dalit literary traditions have deliberately ignored the conventions, customs and practices of their society since they consider such little traditions as having no role in developing a rational society, women writers from these backgrounds considered these traditions as a relevant subject matter in their thematic landscape to give them more validity and authenticity as a testimony. Though it seems to be primitive and irrational, the element of supernatural forms a significant strand in these writings where possession by supernatural forces is a common theme. In the place of male writers who rejected these trivial beliefs and faiths from the mainstream of their narration as part of their overall project to build an enlightened society, women writers incorporated even such elements to give their narration more blood and flesh. For instance, as in these Dalit self-narratives, Morrison's *Beloved* also deals extensively with the theme of supernatural which is vivid through the procedure of exorcism conducted by Ella at the end of the novel to exorcise Beloved, the spirit.

Another significant thematic aspect which binds these writers is their deep desire to document the social and historical reality. Whenever the official historiography fails to accommodate the voice of the marginalized, subaltern literature reassigns its space to include such voices from the margins as part of their overall commitment to the progress of an inclusive humanity. As Barbara Hill Rigney observes in "The Disremembered and Unaccounted For: History, Myth and Magic": "Morrison's novels are historical novels, because they are both subjects of and subject to history, i.e. events in real time, that succession of antagonistic movements that include slavery, reconstruction, depression and war" (61). Similar is the case of Walker's *The Color Purple* which documents the social, cultural and political climate of American South in the early twentieth century. Much passionate expression of political activism and historical consciousness are expressed by the Dalit autobiographers since they believe in the propagandist mission of their writing to challenge the hegemonic forces of exploitation. The commonalities that one can observe in Dalit autobiographies as symbolic representation of their commitment towards the subaltern is the narration of various historical events, social reform movements and historical perspectives. These writings depict the harmonious blend of the personal and the political since its primary concern is to impart voice to the voiceless in the mainstream public discourse. As Baby Kamble writes: "The flame of Bhim started burning in our hearts. We began to walk and talk. We became conscious that we too are human beings. Our eyes began to see and our ears to listen. Blood started coursing through our veins. We got ready to fight as Bhim's soldiers. The struggle yielded us three jewels—humanity, education and the religion of the Buddha" (122).

Though it is unfeasible to equate the social, religious and economic climate of these distinct geographical areas of the world, Black and Dalit literatures share an amazing bond of structural and thematic unity. Their cultural legacy is that of furious protest against social injustice through challenging the hegemonic forces of imperial nature. Moreover, the themes such as shared experience of victimhood, characters with mental and psychological trauma, men of violent chauvinism, issues of identity and race, hypocrisy of institutional religion, question of subaltern women etc. combines these two distinct literary writings into a similar whole. Through unique linguistic and literary diction, they assert their own wounded self which narrates the saga of oppression, suppression and humiliation. Since literature is a mirror to the social, political and cultural realities of life, these writers through their writings encapsulate the societal demonization, devaluation and effective marginalization of the subaltern through recording their mental and psychological trauma. Further, both these literatures constitute the strong and significant voice of subaltern women.

The degradation and dishonour which these women writers suffer as an inferior other in a chauvinistic society structured on the basis of caste and race make their writing more intensive than their male counterparts. The themes of marital rape, child rape and wife-beating as one can easily observe in these writings denote the moral and psychological impact the oppressive ideology has over its victims. The theme of paternal rape that dominates the narrative of Walker and Morrison directs their criticism against the exploitative social order which makes Black men perverts and psychopaths. These abusers are depicted not as one-dimensional devilish figures who are purely evil but as victims of physical and mental violence, thereby giving them both redemption and salvation. At the same time, Dalit autobiography scrutinizes the notion of gender through effectively challenging not only the hypocrisy of Dalit masculinity but also their female counterparts who have internalized the philosophy of patriarchy. As Kamble puts it, "And we too desired to dominate, to wield power. But who would let us do that? So, we made our own arrangements to find slaves—our very own daughters-in-law!" (87).

Another aspect of these writings which interconnect each other is its colloquial language style and the inclusion of traditional customs, myths, folklore, rituals etc. in its thematic space. As Afro-American writers used language experiments in their writing as a tool to regain the lost cultural traditions of their forefathers, Dalit women writers through the use of their own village dialects impart an identity to the language, culture and ritualistic ceremonies of the marginalized. It has the benignity to accommodate diverse literary, artistic and cultural traditions of the voiceless, thereby giving their narrative a more genuine face as realistic expressions of margin lives. It is part of their commitment towards their community, its neglected rituals and customs which have been defaced by the dominant forces of imperial power. For instance, in order to strongly address the issue of caste in Indian Catholic Church, Bama remains close to the vocabulary, proverbs, folk songs and chants of her own *Paraiya* community.

What makes the comparative analysis of Black and Dalit literatures relevant is its twofold impact upon the aesthetic understanding of world literature. On the one hand, it establishes the universal nature of narrative which functions as testimonies of human suffering under institutions of oppression. On the other hand, it works as authentic documents of historiography which describes the strategies and devices of struggle to reclaim human dignity and worth that directly as well as indirectly influences other marginalized groups of the world to assert their identity for social liberation. Hence, it is true to hold that such a comparative study is not only having literary realm but also has cultural and sociological dimensions. As D. Gnaniah puts it: "There are ample grounds to compare and contrast the brief history of the Blacks in USA and the age-long ancient history of misery of Dalits in India. There are numerous similarities of both these black peoples especially in their sufferings and miseries, legal and illegal violence, segregations and ghettoes, whippings and punishments, destitution and hunger, brainwashing and punishments, livelihood, employment, education and culture, denial of entry into Churches and Temples, untouchability and apartheid, housing and civic facilities, suppression and oppression, above all total exclusion from the social order" (3). If one is exploited by the colonial white society, the other is oppressed by the forces of internal colonialism. If one is suffering indignation and humiliation in a foreign land in which their forefathers were sold as slaves, the other is carrying the burden of societal alienation and segregation of staggering magnitude in their own land.

African American literature has always been a source of inspiration for Dalit writers of India, especially for writers from Maharashtra, the cradle of Dalit literary aesthetics. It was Jyoti Rao Phule who for the first time acknowledged the contribution of Americans in the social and political emancipation of Negroes through the dedication of his work *Gulamgiri* to the good people of America. Moreover, a large number of African American writings have been translated into Indian languages by the Dalit writers as part of their solidarity to the global struggles against the forces of oppression. What makes Black literature identical with Dalit literature is its origin rooted in social and cultural movements directed against the hegemonic societal institutions of injustice and tyranny. They share the common legacy of challenging the victimization of humans, not on the basis of their worth but on the basis of their birth. Through rejecting the conventional realms of literary approach, they embraced a unique creative exploration where their deep-rooted sorrows and agonies find its literary expression.

However, there are critics who reject the comparison between African American literature and Dalit literature by suggesting the inherent difference between caste and race. According to them, it is impossible to compare African Americans and Dalits since the formers were never untouchables. As per this theory, untouchability in its actual form can only be considered as denial of humanity. But untouchability in its modern sense is a comprehensive term denoting all sorts of segregation and has an evolving sociological dimension. Hence, it must be acknowledged that their suffering and agony are in no way inferior to that experienced by untouchables of India since both are victims by birth from where there is no escape. Sharankumar Limbale challenges such criticism when he points out: "Dalit literature placed before itself the ideals of African American literature. As a result, this foreign influence gained a stronghold on dalit literature. This is the criticism of Bhausaheb Adsul. To him, this inspiration is 'un-Indian'. Mahatma Phule dedicated his book *Gulamgiri*, to Black people. . . Does this mean that Phule's inspiration was un-Indian?" (Limbale 101)

Though Dalits of India never suffered official form of slavery as African Americans did, they were victims of informal slavery both physical and mental. Their legacy is that of continuous misery and destitution which have been normalized in their existence. Even till the beginning of twentieth century they were denied basic human and social rights in the name of caste. As Shivaji Sergar observes, "Until recently, they were denied the right to education; they were forced to live outside the villages; and the public places and temples were closed for them. The monster of segregation was all powerful, discrimination among the people on the basis of their caste." In conclusion we can say that the legacies of both African American and Indian Dalit are analogous to each other both in life and literature since their emotional worlds are rooted in similar social circumstances. There are significant commonalities in their protests and hopes since both are fighting for human dignity and social rights. Though they are miles apart both geographically and culturally, they share an unbreakable bond of victimhood which makes them identical twins of tragic legacy both in life and literature.

Works Cited

Gates Jr., Henry Louis, ed. "Introduction." *Reading Black, Reading Feminist: A Critical Anthology*. New York: Meridian, 1990.

Gnaniah, D. *Obamas of America and Dalits of India--Saga of Two Black People*, New Delhi, Pragun, 2011.

Kamble, Baby. *The Prisons We Broke*, trans. Maya Pandit. Chennai: Orient Longman, 2008.

Limbale, Sharan Kumar. *Towards an Aesthetic of Dalit Literature*. New Delhi: Orient Longman, 2004.

Mangai. "Bama." *Storylines: Conversation with Women Writers*, ed. Ammu Joseph et.al. Delhi: Women's World, 2003. 111-20.

Rege, Sharmila. *Writing Caste/ Writing Gender: Narrating Dalit Women's Testimonios*. New Delhi: Zubaan, 2006.

Rigney, Barbara Hill. "The Disremembered and Unaccounted For: History, Myth and Magic." *The Voices of Toni Morrison*. Columbus: Ohio University Press, 1991: 61-81.

Schreiber, Evelyn Jaffe. *Race, Trauma, and Home in the Novels of Toni Morrison*. Louisiana State University Press, 2010.

Sergar, Shivaji. "African American and Dalit Autobiography," *The Criterion, An International Journal in English*, Vol III, Issue II.

Walker, Alice. "In Search of Our Mothers' Gardens." *Womanist Prose*. Florida: Harcourt, 1983.

Writing the Difference: Subaltern Narrative of Anand Neelakantan's *Asura*

ARPAN ADHIKARY
Ph.D. Res. Sch., University of Burdwan

The obliterated, obscured history and denigrated myth of the Asura tribe of the ancient India are evoked and given a critical space in Neelakantan's novel *Asura: Tale of the Vanquished* (2012) which delineates in the safe paradigm of fiction the instances of what Spivak calls the "epistemic violence" against the Asuras by the Devas meted out through "the remotely orchestrated, far-flung, and heterogeneous project to constitute the colonial subject as Other" as well as "the asymmetrical obliteration of the trace of that Other in its precarious Subjectivity" (1994: 76). The Devas' metanarratives of victory over the Asuras, especially, the *Puranas* and the epic *Ramayana*, prioritize and legitimize the victor-colonizer's point of view, and thereby present the vanquished Asuras as mean and evil, suppressing and nullifying their utterances of the alternative versions of the stories of the socio-political battles through which the Devas spread their empire destroying that of the Asuras. The stories of the ostracized Asuras remained underground ever since, un-archived and unauthorized, manifest only in obscure fragments in the collective unconscious of certain tribes. Neelakantan ventures to use the platform of fiction for a comprehensive and dialectical critique of the polyphonic possibilities of an "Asurayana" or "Ravanayana" that will serve to rupture the hegemony of the grand narrative of the *Ramayana*, the revered epic of the privileged class, whose myths and metaphors are prone to be taken at face value and confused with reality by a vast majority of readers even today.

The narrativization of the tales of the vanquished and the dead as deconstructive subtexts of the *Ramayana* approximates the mode of Derridean *ghostwriting*. The "apparition of the inapparent"[1] is skilfully conjured up in this novel by means of a highly stylized work of mourning in which the figures of Ravana and Bhadra are left to recount their stories of defeat, destitution and death "in an attempt to establish the ethical relation with history as such" (Spivak 1995: 70). Spivak notes that what is ethical "is not a problem of knowledge but a problem of relation. It is singular yet generalizable" and that out of such ethical obligation one craves to be haunted by history "as a ghost or ghosts, with the ungraspable incorporation of a ghostly body, and the uncontrollable, sporadic, and unanticipatable periodicity of haunting" (*Ibid.* 70). Neelakantan's ethical responsibility to the otherized Asuras is manifest in the hauntological resurrection of not only the prominent figure of Ravana, the antagonist of the *Ramayana*, but a nondescript figure like Bhadra, in an effort "to compute with the software of other pasts . . . for the sake of the politics of identitarian competition" (*Ibid.* 70).The vanquished Asuras—whose true identity and history remained in apparent and obfuscated in the grand narrative of the vanquisher—are conjured up by Neelakantan in an effort to narrativize what Spivak calls "the continuing construction of the subaltern" (1994: 90).

The conjured up narratorial apparitions of the Asuras operate as what Derrida calls "the autonomized idea or thought" (2006: 158). According to Derrida, this autonomized thought is the spirit whose incarnation induces the spectrogenic process of "paradoxical incorporation" dissipating into alienation, simulation, expropriation and supplementation of the spectre (157-58). Neelakantan's novel, which begins with 'The End' and averts narrative closure by ending with 'The Beginning,' performs *ghostwriting* through the precise incorporation of the writer's autonomized thought with shrewd subaltern consciousness into the resurrected narratorial bodies of Ravana and Bhadra, thereby initiating the spectral articulation and the intricate play of alienation, expropriation and supplementation to the decline and fall of the hegemony of the metanarrative of the *Ramayana*. In the unconventional 'About the Author' section, written in first-person, Neelakantan predisposes the narrative discourse of haunting:

> But the Asura Emperor would not leave me alone. For six years he haunted my dreams, walked with me, and urged me to write his version of the story. He was not the only one who wanted his version of the story to be told. One by one, irrelevant and minor characters of the *Ramayana* kept coming up with their own versions. . . . This is then *Asurayana*, the story of the Asuras, the story of the vanquished. (4)

The hauntological paradigm of the narrative renders this novel a *cryptomimetic* work that is "predicated upon haunting, mourning, and the return of the so-called living dead" (Castricano 32). As Jodey Castricano explains, in *cryptomimesis*[2] the "structuring principle is abjection" and a *cryptomimetic* work "approaches abjection" by concerning itself "with the collapse, or the permeability, of the border between inside and outside, between attraction and repulsion" (32). Neelakantan's novel exemplifies this tenet. The writer, being haunted by the spectres of the vanquished Asuras, experiences the similar abjection that characterizes the figures like Ravana and Bhadra. The narrative mimesis of the *crypted* entities and desires of the defeated and the dead confuses and defamiliarizes the demarcations between the notions of the right and the wrong, the heroic and the villainous, the good and the evil, as standardized by the metanarratives of the vanquisher, and thereby this subaltern narrative potentially destabilizes the reader's preconceived responses of attraction and repulsion as to certain epic personalities.

The spectres of the dead Asuras like Ravana and Bhadra thus haunt the writer because, as Nicolas Abraham notes, "all the departed may return, but some are destined to haunt: the dead who were shamed during their lifetime or those who took unspeakable secrets to the grave" (171). This is particularly true of both the cases of Ravana and Bhadra. They haunt because they want to express what they could not in their lifetime "having suffered repression" and unable to "enjoy, even in death, a state of authenticity"; and they haunt not as mere dead entities, but as spectral manifestations of what Abraham calls "the gaps left within us by the secrets of others" (171). The narrative of "Asurayana" practises at length the task of "being-with" spectres, which Derrida calls "a *politics* of memory, of inheritance, and of generations" and considers to be "necessary" when one needs to speak of, to and with the ghost "in the name of *justice*" (xviii). With the question of justice, Derrida attaches the crucial issues of respect and responsibility which one must have:

> the ghosts of those who are not yet born or who are already dead, be they victims of wars, political or other kinds of violence, nationalist, racist, colonialist, sexist, or other kinds of exterminations, victims of the oppressions of capitalist imperialism or any of the forms of totalitarianism. (2006: xviii)

Neelakantan's *ghostwriting* of the subaltern narrative of defeat and death exudes ethical concern for justice for such victims of political, racist and sexist exterminations as Bali, Hiranyakshpa, Ravana, Bhadra and Sita among numerous others whose absent presence haunts the writer and ruptures the metaphysics of presence that his consciousness had been preoccupied with, thus inducing his abjection which sustains and validates the subaltern discourse of this *cryptomimetic* tale. As Julia Kristeva observes, "fear having been bracketed, discourse will seem tenable only if it ceaselessly confront that otherness, a burden both repellent and repelled, a deep well of memory that is unapproachable and intimate: the abject." (6)

While the burden of the forgotten and obfuscated tales of the vanquished is repelled by the hegemonic normativity of the epic *Ramayana*, it also becomes repellent to it by the potential of spectrogenic supplementation. The narrative discourse of this novel strikes the note of dialectical feasibility by steadily encountering the problematics of other-ness evoked by the memory and abjection of the spectres that the writer is haunted by and finds affinity with.

The narrative of *Asura* implies that since "the subaltern cannot speak" (1994: 104) from its essentially suppressed and silenced position under the discursive hegemony of the oppressor, it must express itself through haunting. The writer poses himself as a scribe serving on behalf of the spectres of the Others that haunt him with their respective tales of abjection. It is these tales of abjection narrated by the spectral personas of Ravana and Bhadra that the novel consists of, rather than an elaborate mourning for the defeated and the deceased, since "the ghost comes back because what is buried is untellable and, therefore, (necessarily) inaccessible to the gradual, painful, assimilative work of mourning" (Castricano 36). However, the problem with the arrangement of these tales in a proper narrative framework is that, as Castricano argues, "the crypt effect is one of continuous displacement in which the vacillating undecidability of one's position contributes to a reading and a writing of the text of the *other*" (102). This is how the ethical standpoints as well as the moods and the motives of Ravana and Bhadra, as corresponded through the narration of a haunted scribe who shares their abjection, appear to be in constant flux deterring the normative tendency of binary typification. Such ideological flux lies at the heart of *ghostwriting* which is necessarily dialectical in nature and seeks to accommodate multiplicity of perspectives, since "to play hauntologically . . . is not only to acknowledge that multiple perspectives exist, but to purposely create spaces in our work where they might emerge and/ or insert themselves" (Powell and Shaffer 2).

Neelakantan's subaltern subtext of the *Ramayana* thus becomes a *bricolage* of diverse ways of seeing, not only those of the two storytellers Ravana and Bhadra, but of several other figures who feature in the recollections and narratives of these two. The assimilative accommodation of different perspectives undermines the normative monopoly of the epic of the vanquisher, and constitutes an alternative body of writing whose decentred, permuted and flexible form allows for the *free play*[3] of signifiers. A remarkable point of this narrative is that though it denounces and ruptures the hegemony of the *Ramayana*, it does not eulogize Ravana or any of the Asura figures it features. Neelakantan's aim is merely to let the subaltern speak out the other possible versions of a grand narrative so that at least a dialectical confrontation among different discursive domains may take place. The figure of Ravana embodies and epitomizes the dichotomies that mar the race of Asuras. Still, he gains significance as a potential subversive ploy against the ideological and axiomatic constructs of the Brahminical systems of oppression through his shrewd critiques that lay bare the hypocrisies of the Brahminical rhetoric concerning apotheosis, spirituality and morality. Ravana's voice evokes a strong subaltern consciousness about the difference, the other-ness, possessed by the Asura tribes in matters of ethnic identity and socio-political systems as he proudly asserts:

> Our sense of justice differed from what the learned and the privileged considered right. We decided our righteousness and we defined our rights in our own way. We learned that the truth could be bent to suit one's needs. . . . We never knew any of the great teachings of the ancient Asura or Deva saints. We followed no tradition. We were almost bastards. (17)

The awareness of the difference between the ruler and the ruled also leads to Ravana's proletarian understanding of the stark reality of widespread social oppression and exploitation of the Asuras by the Devas. He tells,

> wherever I looked, I only saw oppression. Money, caste, rituals, traditions, beliefs and superstitions all conspired together to crush the humble majority. . . . The moment I started asking *why*, I was branded a hothead. The Brahmin friends of my father once tried to banish me from the village saying I was possessed by evil spirits and that I was a *Rakshasa*, a demon. (19)

This astutely summarizes the Devas' strategic project of otherizing the Asuras while vilifying and suppressing the voices of opposition. Ravana recounts that in opposition to the rigorously caste-bound hierarchy of the Deva society, "the Asuras were a casteless society and had a highly democratic set up where an elected council, instead of a king, held actual power" (21). Ravana's view on divinity is also very pragmatic. Stating that he is "no atheist," Ravana claims that for him, "God is a very personal thing and prayer needs to be spoken silently in [one's] heart" (20). What he looks down upon is the Brahminical diplomacy of apotheosis by which the Devas claimed and legitimized their supremacy. He shrewdly observes how, over centuries, the prosperous kingdoms and civilizations of the Nagas, the Kinnaras, the Yakshas and the Gandharvas were strategically obliterated by the atrocious Deva-rule, and the "spin-doctors of the conquerors" succeeded in "ascribing divinity to their own leaders" who were "bad rulers and pitiful administrators" (22-23).

Ravana understands that in order to free his nations from the Deva rule he must first of all categorically undermine the fundamental axioms of the Brahminical institutions, since he cannot win the battle fighting by the enemy's rules as Mahabali does in vain. His proclamation of his identity as Dasamukha is a blow at the roots of the axiomatic constructs of the Brahminical social system, as well as an assertion of the subaltern identity of the Other whose ethical values differ from those standardized by the vanquisher-ruler. Refuting the assimilative value-education of the Devas that Mahabali fell prey to, Ravana asserts,

> My aim is neither to become God nor achieve moksha. At best I think, those are old wives' tales. . . . I shall live like a man and die as one. I will never try to be a God. I will live exactly as my emotions tell me to. I do not want to be a model man for future generations to follow. My life begins and ends with me. (41)

The point to note is that after having his lessons from Mahabali and Brahma, Ravana does not disrespect the great philosophical precepts of the Vedas; what he seeks to refute and subvert are the manipulative maxims of Brahminical ethics which are used to tame the rebellious and denigrate the deviators. Ravana's acute subaltern consciousness helps him see through the Devas' tactics to establish their racial and cultural superiority by enforcing their social and moral codes supplanting and vilifying those of the Asuras, and he sarcastically notes, "it is perhaps the Deva's burden to civilize us" (73).

The novel, however, does not prioritize a linear perspective like that of Ravana, who, despite being a subaltern figure, becomes an autocratic ruler and his views and ways are subject to criticism by the other "insignificant, irrelevant and dumb nobodies" (494) like Bhadra and Mala, whose marginal situation in the society enables them to closely scrutinize the socio-political systems and moral foibles of not only the invading Devas, but the indigenous races such as the Asuras and the Gandharvas. From her position of a courtesan, Mala blurts:

> I do not care for any king. They are all the same. What is so fancy about the new one [Ravana]? Deva, Asura, Gandharva, half-castes, they are all the same. They only worry about how to glue their fat asses to the throne and screw the people. They talk big, like the

> emancipation of the Asuras, getting even with the Devas, preservation of culture, and all that humbug. (130)

Such a trenchant critique from one belonging to the lower strata of society invalidates the scope of designating the "Ravanayana" as an alternative epic glorifying a subaltern anti-hero. These kinds of observations abound in the narrative, and effectively disrupt the illusion of an alternative epic of the Asuras. The *play* of so many subaltern perspectives renders the narrative of *Asura* polyphonic and multi-dimensional, resisting and refuting the epical norms of linear narration and hero-worship.

Neelakantan's *ghostwriting* in *Asura* adds a new tinge to the varied spectrum of themes and narrative techniques of the subaltern literature. The mythical subject is contemporized with the use of modern narrative techniques that problematize a redundant grand narrative by evoking debatable subtextual issues of present pertinence. The astute use of the discourse of haunting validates the fusion of postcolonial and deconstructive perspectives in a subaltern narrative that critiques and ruptures the linearity and hegemony of the epical narrative of the vanquisher. This novel exemplifies how the subaltern can actually speak and how the alternative narrative of the subaltern can defamiliarize the mystified map of myth-reading.

NOTES

1. "Apparition of the Inapparent" is the title of the fifth chapter of Derrida's book *Spectres of Marx*. In this chapter Derrida elaborates the "spectrogenic process" of incorporation of, and, in-between the spirit and the body. The phrase is here used in connection with Neelakantan's rendition of a *ghostwriting* in which the inapparent and suppressed figures of the epic appear as apparitions to disrupt the axiomatic constructs of the narrative hegemony of the epic.
2. Jodey Castricano in her book *Cryptomimesis* uses this term to refer to "a writing practice that is characterized by disintegration" with

especial connection to the style of Derridean ghost writing which relies on "the aesthetic principle" of "decomposition" (32).

3. Derrida in his essay "Structure, Sign and Play in the Discourse of the Human Sciences" argues that when a structure, narrative or epistemological, is decentred, the "structurality of the structure" becomes disorganized and the infinite "free play" of signifiers initiates.

Works Cited

Abraham, Nicolas. "Notes on the Phantom: A Complement to Freud's Metapsychology," *The Shell and the Kernel: Renewals of Psychoanalysis*, vol. 1, Nicolas Abraham and Maria Torok, ed. and trans. Nicholas T. Rand, Chicago and London, University of Chicago Press, 1994, pp. 171-76.

Castricano, Jodey. *Cryptomimesis: The Gothic and Jacques Derrida's Ghost Writing*. Montreal and Kingston, McGill-Queen's University Press, 2001.

Derrida, Jacques. *Specters of Marx: The State of the Debt, the Work of Mourning and the New International*, trans. Peggy Kamuf, New York and London, Routledge, 2006.

_____. "Structure, Sign and Play in the Discourse of the Human Sciences." *Writing and Difference*, trans. Alan Bass, London and New York, Routledge, 2001.

Kristeva, Julia. *Powers of Horror: An Essay on Abjection*, trans. Leon S. Roudiez, New York, Columbia University Press, 1982.

Neelakantan, Anand. *Asura: Tale of the Vanquished*. Mumbai, Platinum Press, 2017.

Powell, Benjamin D. and Tracy Stephenson Shaffer. "On the Haunting of Performance Studies," *Liminalities: A Journal of Performance Studies*, vol. 5, no. 1, April 2009, pp. 1-19.

Spivak, Gayatri Chakravorty. "Can the Subaltern Speak?" *Colonial Discourse and Postcolonial Theory: A Reader*, ed. Patrick Williams and Laura Chrisman, New York, Columbia University Press, 1994, pp. 66-111.

_____. "Ghostwriting." *Diacritics*, vol. 25, no. 2, Summer 1995, pp. 64-84.

Feminist Perspective in Alice Walker's *The Color Purple*

SEEMANT
Kanya Mahavidyalaya, Kharkhoda, Sonipat

Feminist criticism is a mode of critical discourse that takes into account the culturally determined gender differences. It generally focuses on the alienating effects of phallocentrism reflected in society and literature. To dismantle the bases of phallocentrism and reductionist aesthetic, feminist criticism denounces patriarchal supremacist values, masculinist assumptions and male domination. Black feminist critics have also established an integral relationship between the author and the text.

The Color Purple is a 1982 epistolary novel by American author Alice Walker which won the 1983 Pulitzer Prize for Fiction. Taking place mostly in Georgia, the story focuses on the life of African American women in the southern United States in the 1930s, addressing numerous issues including their exceedingly low position in American social culture. It focuses on minority ethnic group, existing on the fringes of the elitist white culture. Black feminism relates racial politics to the issues of self-identity, patriarchy gender and class in the context of modernism and postmodernism.

The novel unfolds the panorama of black female reality of the neo-slavery period that takes shape in the smithy of black male brutality towards black females, racial/patriarchal oppression and misogynist assumptions. It focuses on the process of self-discovery of an unlettered black southern woman. It traces the gradual growth of her radicalization and empowerment through female bonding, education and self-employment. The black feminist analysis reveals how black female radicalism, embracing of womanhood, exploration of black heritage and resultant self-determination bring to fruition Celie's quest for identity and history.

Celie succeeds in her quest for identity and history by developing an understanding of her roots and heritage and acquiring the awareness that she has a right to happiness, passion, creativity and emotional fulfilment. To exercise her rights as an individual, Celie learns to resist the advances of black men who hinder her self-fulfilment. Alice Walker has been vehemently criticized within the African American community for her portrayal of black men as abusers and rapists. In *The Color Purple*, Walker establishes a "feminist culture" by focusing attention on the underprivileged and inconspicuous southern black woman, who suffers not only at the hands of the white society but also due to black male oppression. The adverse criticism of the theme of black male brutality in *The Color Purple* seeks legitimacy from the belief that the patriarchal practice of sexist politics symbolizes black opposition to racial oppression. Thus, the black male aggression against black woman is camouflaged as reaction to social victimization.

Bell Hooks regards this perspective on black male brutality as an expression of the pedagogy of patriarchy and rhetoric of Black Nationalism which collaborate in oppressing the black woman. Albert, Celie's malevolent husband, embodies the black male chauvinism and the patriarchal assumptions and tendencies, analyzed by Bell Hooks. In the absence of another benevolent black male character, he seems to represent the majority of black American manhood. Alice Walker has refuted the allegation that she has presented Albert in order to tarnish the image of black men in general and create a schism between black men and women. Besides establishing the interlinkages of race and gender in *The Color Purple*, Alice Walker reinforces her position as a "womanish" writer. Despite being labelled a womanish text, *The Color Purple* does not fall into a specific genre category. It represents the "blurring of genre conventions." Alice Walker reinterprets the genres and uses them in a postmodernist sense, diverse from the traditional practice. It strikes us as an epistolary novel, a *bildungsroman* and a historical novel all in one.

The Color Purple adopts the narrative technique of the eighteenth century epistolary novel of sentiment. The epistolary form enables Celie, a black southern woman to speak for herself. By writing letters, Celie discovers a means of structuring her identity and discovering herself. The novel unfolds itself in "the process of Celie's writing herself into being and consciousness, of her growing power and control as a writer" (Bloom 185). The novel's narrative structure is closely linked to the theme of search for identity and history. The ingenuity of Alice Walker lies in revising the genre conventions of the sentimental novel. Alice Walker unfolds the narrative of the novel through a series of letters, which are not dated and numbered. It is a device, aiming at preserving the verisimilitude of the narrative. The letters, written by Celie and her sister, Nettie, reveal political consciousness and throw light on the contemporary, social, political and cultural scenario.

Due to the peculiarities of the epistolary form, the novel demands to be read intensively. Clues and hints within the letters reveal the social set up of the period. In the opening letters, there are references to wagons and the closing letters reveal the appearance of cars. The time span of the novel is roughly about forty years. There are also large time spans between the letters, sometimes of about five years. The epistolary form has enabled Alice Walker to press into service the resources of a western tradition for exploiting the creativity of African American folk expression. In this regard, David Bloom makes an apt observation: "Celie's letters transpose a black and oral mode into a western epistolary tradition. Walker's use of the vernacular has invested an old and somewhat rigid form with new life" (Bloom 68).

The Color Purple records the voice of Celie, an illiterate southern black woman, who is raped by her stepfather and then married to Mr. Johnson, who could make use of a good worker on his farm. Threatened by her stepfather that she had better tell no one but God about her rape at his hands, Celie starts writing letters to God, The entire novel comprises Celie's letters to God, then to her sister Nettie, and of Nettie's letters to Celie. After her children are separated from Celie and her sister Nettie escapes the advances of Mr. Johnson and leaves for Africa with missionaries, Celie sinks into isolation. With the passage of time, she develops affinity with an extended family which includes Shug, her husband's mistress who is a juke joint singer and the strong and rebellious Sofia. With the help of the black sisterhood, Celie overcomes oppression and acquires an identity and a sense of her history. In the end, Nettie and Celie's children are reunited with Celie. Mr. Johnson mellows down and develops respect for Celie and her new-found independence.

Celie's evolution of self is slow and gradual. Her journey to self-realization is a long and arduous one. Linda Tate contends that Celie's transformation stems from her "ability to take control over defining oneself, naming oneself" (204). In the beginning, Celie is a mere "nothing." Mr. Johnson rebukes her: "Who you think you is? . . . You black, you pore, you ugly, you a woman. Goddamn, . . . you nothing at all" (Dieke 164). At this stage, Celie accepts Mr. Johnson's contention that she is a mere "nothing." She lives a desolate existence. She cannot even begin her narrative by stating, "I am" due to lack of self-confidence and self-acceptance. As a result, Celie suffers silently and passively. As a result of her silence in the face of oppression, "Celie has been fragmented into pieces which are given away to others" (Dieke 164). Her life is a series of sacrifices to her father's ruthless desires, to her sister's safety, and to Mr. Johnson's cruelty.

She leads a devastated, hopeless life after being abused by her father and her husband and her separation from her children and her sister. She lacks a sense of belonging and self.

As the novel evolves, Celie gradually moves towards self-acceptance and later self-assertion. She asserts herself for the first time when she takes the decision, on her own behalf, of leaving for Memphis with Shug. She boldly announces her existence on earth, "I'm pore, I'm black, I may be ugly and can't cook. . . . But I'm here" (205). In Memphis, Celie, for the first time, gives expression to her dormant potential and creativity. In a letter, written to Nettie, from Memphis, Celie communicates a new and positive vision of herself: "I am so happy. I got love, I got work, I got money, friends and time. And you alive and be home soon. With our children." Furthermore, Celie, for the first time at the close of this letter, signs emphatically, thereby revealing her new sense of self that she has acquired through her relationships and her business:

> Your sister, Celie
> Folkpants, Unlimited
> Sugar Avery Drive,
> Memphis, Tennessee. (212)

Celie comes close to acquiring a sense of identity in Memphis, which opens up new vistas for her and brings her in contact with the world at large. From newspapers, Celie learns about global happenings. It is significant that Celie is reborn in Georgia. Her discovery of self in the south marks her wholesome acceptance of the south and all that it represents. By returning to the south, Celie acquires a sense of belonging and roots. The import of the theme of black sisterhood in *The Color Purple* can be fully understood only in the southern perspective.

At the end of the novel, Nettie and Celie's children also return to the sustaining south. Celie's experiencing extreme joy and fulfilment after reunion with her long-separated family marks the final step in her quest for identity. Alice Walker has been criticized for the unrealistic, fairytale ending of the novel. The ending of the novel "creates a utopia vision of new southern community" (Perkins 127). However, the ending of the novel is also redemptive as the celebration in the end makes up for the misery with which the novel begins. Nettie and Celie's children return home to Georgia, their "mothers' gardens" to seek integration with the community from which they sprang. Celie's reunion with her family coincides with the American Independence Day. As white Americans celebrate their independence from England, black Americans spend the day celebrating each other. In a clever twist, Alice Walker uses this traditionally white holiday to mark the emotional, social, economic and spiritual independence of Celie.

The Color Purple, an odd miracle of nature, symbolizes the miracle of human possibilities. Celie succeeds in her quest for an identity because she recognizes the strength of the south, integrates with her race and refuses to internalize the alienating influences of the western white tradition. Celie's evolution from a self-effacing woman to a woman whose consciousness allows her to gain control over her life is inspiring. Celie however would not have been able to attain a sense of self entirely by herself. Nettie, Shug and Sofia who form a close sisterhood aid her in her quest for identity. In this context, *The Color Purple* focuses on southern black female survival and transcendence. In *The Color Purple*, Alice Walker clearly "lays out for us the theme that dominates her work continuity and creativity in southern black women's lives" (Wade 88). "Sister's choice" is the pattern of the quilt Celie and Sofia create together. The quilt becomes a symbol of the "female bonding that restores the women to a sense of completeness and independence" (Inge 320). Quilting together creates a well-knit female community in a world that represses female expression.

Besides dealing with Celie's self-discovery, *The Color Purple* also focuses on Celie's quest for history. In this sense, it is also a historical novel that chronicles Celie's coming to terms with the legacy of her race and her roots. It affirms and makes black history. It traces the history of the blacks from Africa to the suburbs of the USA. The novel captures Celie's developing a sense of her racial roots and history. Celie's distinct identity is defined by her transformation from a meek subservient woman into an angry and assertive woman. She wants to kill Mr. Johnson for concealing Nettie's letters from her and thus blocking her channel of communication with her sister. Nettie dissuades her from taking recourse to violence and persuades her to be tolerant. Moreover she imparts the liberating knowledge of their racial legacy to Celie and enthuses her to emerge successful in her quest for history. Thus, by tapping the creativity of the epistolary form, Alice Walker has "created an internal dialogue, comparing and contrasting, and finally reconciling poor and middle class, educated and uneducated, African and Afro-American heritage. Nettie's letters to Celie constitute the sub-text of the novel. From vastly different points of view . . . the two sisters gradually come to identical realizations about the nature of life, blackness, and men and women" (Wade 96-97).

Celie attains this happiness by reconciling with the past. In the process, she also helps others like Albert to make peace with their surroundings. Like her prominent African American predecessors, Jean Toomer and Zora Neale Hurston, Alice Walker focuses on black female identity and wholeness. In this sense, the impact of *The Color Purple* on African American literature and culture has been abiding.

The black feminist approach also underlines the opposition of men to the emancipation of women and the varying responses of the male and female characters to the emerging social order, which enables women to assert themselves and gain economic independence. It focuses on the existential project of the female characters in the novel and brings into focus their womanish slant and exclusion of men from their sisterhood and struggle for self-realization and empowerment.

Works Cited

Bloom, Harold. *A Map of Misreading.* New York: Oxford University Press, 1975.

Dieke, Ikenna, ed. *Critical Essays on Alice Walker.* London: Greenwood Press, 1999.

Inge, Tonettc Bond, ed. *Black, Southern, Womanist: The Genius of Alice Walker. Southern Women Writers. The New Generation.* London: The University of Alabama Press, 2004.

Walker, Alice. *The Third Life of Grange Copeland.* New York: Harcourt Brace Jovanovich, 1970.

_____. *The Color Purple.* New York: Washington Square Press, 1982.

_____. *In Search of Our Mothers' Gardens.* San Diego: Harcourt Brace Jovanovich, 1983.

Diaspora, Long Distance Nationalism and Globalization

TRIPADA BHARATI
L.S College, Muzaffarpur

As the etymology of the word 'diaspora' suggests (dia means about, across; sperein means to scatter) it has been associated with the notions of pain, exile and longing for repatriation to its origins. Much of its weight has been derived from the classic example of Jewish dispersion that was forced to be dispersed across the world in the sixth century B.C. However, as we steered into modern postcolonial world, the word started to gain a progressive secularization. In this broader context, as described by Safran, "diaspora community" includes, "expatriates, expellees, political refugees, alien residents, immigrants and ethnic and racial minorities tout court" (83). Besides, the development in the sociological theories in 1960s (postmodernism, Cultural Studies, Deconstruction) countered the essentialism of oneness and instead argued for multiplicity and a movement from centre to its periphery. This development nicely fitted into diaspora, leading to its emergence from the pathological condition of pain and exile to a healthy one which is open to embracing diversity and multiculturalism. (Dufoix 1367)

As one of the typical characteristics of diaspora, the myth of the return is quite a contentious yet sustainable one. Stuart Hall argues, "It is not a fixed origin to which we can make some final and absolute Return. Of course, it is not a mere phantasm either. . . . It has its histories—or histories have their real material and symbolic affects" (226). He builds up his case of cultural identity for diaspora emphasizing the fact that diasporic history of the past can't be dismissed. Past with its paraphernalia of 'memory, fantasy narrative and myth' helps diaspora in forging a meaningful relation and consequently engaging with its homeland in a mutually beneficial way. Diaspora, thus, gains distinctive cultural identity, challenges the homogenizing forces of assimilation of the adopted land, and harbours nationalistic feeling for its motherland.

Benedict Anderson rightly analyses the psyche of diaspora saying it is painful for diaspora to be stuck in hyphenated identities. Being politically marginalized and economically subordinated, there are practically hundreds of reasons; their political psychology often remains nostalgically oriented towards their "heimat" or their places of origin (9). Anderson has famously coined the phrase for such tendencies which he calls "Long Distance Nationalism." As Nina Glick Schiller writes: "National borders are not thought to delimit membership in the nation. The members of the nation may live anywhere around the globe and even hold citizenship in other states. This does not, in view of the long distant nationalists, abrogate the relationship between members of the nation and their national homeland. Long-distance nationalists are expected to maintain some kind of loyalty to homeland and on the basis of this attachment take whatever action the homeland requires. The nature of these actions varies depending on the political and economic situation of the homeland." (571)

Carrying the burden of the past, the diaspora inevitably imagines its belonging to its 'home' (Nation State). This sense of belonging in fact gives rise to 'Long-Distance Nationalism' in diaspora which manifests itself in various ways. It has been ubiquitously seen that diaspora organizes socio-cultural projects to promote the common interests of the diasporic community thereby reinforcing its bonding with the Home-State. Their actions can range from organizing socio-cultural projects to demonstrating, lobbying, contributing money, sometimes culminating in the realization of the extreme end of killing and dying.

Long Distance Nationalism is not a new phenomenon, so to speak. It can be safely assumed that it is as old as the phenomenon of exile as histories speak of the role of political exiles in building up the nationalist movement. Germany, Hungary, Italy, Brazil, Ireland and several other countries have maintained transnational political connections long before the concept of Long Distance Nationalism came into existence. The term used for such participation in the home country politics by diaspora in the first half of the twentieth century was referred to as 'home country nationalism'. Even the independence struggle for colonized countries like India, Kenya and Vietnam was built up effectively by intellectuals residing away from their homelands (Schiller 572).

With the advent of globalization in the late twentieth century, Nation States became its chief actors as well as partakers. It led to a positive engagement between Nation-States through a set of international commerce policies. However, it led to diminished role for some and exalted roles for others according to the economic potential of the countries. In addition, globalization strengthened diaspora like never before. Coupled with internet revolution, it played an instrumental role in bringing the latent 'Long Distance Nationalism' in diaspora to the fore. Not only did it facilitate easy physical mobility but also the transfer of information in a jiffy championed by digitalization of media. The liminal identity of diaspora acquired positive connotation in terms of fluid identity in the context of global transnational, multicultural world. Given this scenario, it does seem likely that globalization and its fetish for market is doing away with the borders of Nation State. However, the paper contends that globalization, transnationalism and nationalist processes are not mutually exclusive and contradictory in nature.

They should rather be seen as complementing each other. In fact, the whole paradigm of Long Distance Nationalism is dependent on its adaptation to the modern means of communication as in internet, cyberspace and social media.

Nevertheless some scholars believed Long Distance Nationalism as ephemeral first generation diaspora phenomenon and saw multiculturalism as an answer for the craving for the lost homeland. The two World Wars of the twentieth century and the quite long Cold War greatly disrupted the transnational ties and the feelings of Long Distance Nationalism among the immigrant population. However in many cases, it has been seen that government has itself encouraged Long Distance Nationalism. America fanned Long Distance Nationalism among its immigrants from countries under Soviet Union such as Georgia, Estonia, Latvia, in order to counter the gigantic forces of Soviet Union (Schiller 573).The forces of modernization towards the closing of 20th century saw a huge upsurge of immigrant populations in developed countries such as America, Europe and the Gulf. Global economy was reconstituted under the forces of capitalistic free market policy assisted by new technological and digital advancements. Immigrants were now in a better position to keep their ties with the homeland. No doubt, it contributed to the rise in the phenomenon of latent Long Distance Nationalism in diaspora. The global interconnectedness facilitated by internet counterparts like Facebook, Twitter and other potent digital media has led to an unprecedented rise in youth mobility under the rubric of long distance nationalism. It's but natural that expatriate communities are nicely integrated in their national landscape now.

The present-day diasporic communities are in a better position to contribute positively and significantly to their homelands. Diaspora's engagement with the homeland in terms of investments and remittances for the well-being of families in the countries of their origin are significant in this regard.

Besides, diaspora entrepreneurs are also contributing to the socio-economic development of their home countries by generating jobs and businesses, hence, creating broader social capital and financial capital towards development. Countries with big burgeoning diaspora such as India have relaxed their laws in order to foster a healthy and mutually beneficial relationship with their diaspora. Dual nationality, dual citizenship laws, external voting etcetera are some of the means by which nation states are trying to rebuild their relationship with diaspora. The government of India in 2003 amended 1955 citizenship act to extend dual citizenship to certain people designated by Indian governments as "People of Indian Origin" (PIO). This new legislation about dual citizenship, however, benefits only a limited Indian diaspora: Indians who are settled in United States, Britain, Australia, Canada, Finland, Ireland, the Netherlands and Italy. The Indian government has also been observing Pravasi Bhartiya Diwas every year on 9th January since its inception in 2003, to commemorate the return of Mahatma Gandhi to India from South Africa. This annual celebration by Indian government by The Ministry of External Affairs, apart from strengthening diaspora homeland ties, showcases opportunities for diaspora to invest in India. Nation states fuelling Long Distance Nationalism now see diaspora as one of their assets and as an important resource. Long distance nationalism clearly has its partakers in Nation States as well as in diaspora.

Indeed, globalization facilitated the engagement between diaspora and Nation-States, yet there were scholars who believed that globalization may lead to the demise of nation states. It was argued that free market leading to the free flow of people, goods and information across borders have made the borders porous. Stephane Dufoix argues that this porosity is not detrimental to the nation-state. He further clarifies: "If the globalization process is an open spatialization of economic, political, cultural and social relations, it also encompasses state capacities to go beyond their border. . . . The nation extends its limits beyond state borders and the very definitions of the nation and nationality are being transformed since not only citizens abroad, but also former citizens or descendents of former citizens, still belong to the nation" (1374-75). Indubitably, globalization with its technical-digital advancements played a major role in bridging gap between diaspora and Nation State in a positive way.

However, on the one hand globalization eroded certain geo-political boundaries; on the other it inevitably created new boundaries while mutually reinforcing each other in the process. Diasporic nationalism is largely projected as defensive project. The rationale behind it is that cross border ethno-mobilization is needed in order to ensure ethnic-political boundaries which are under constant threat. The participant enjoys the fervour of nationalism while sitting in his safe transnational abode away from the risky stratcgics of thc homcland. Thc anonymous world of digital space in fact facilitates such "unaccountable nationalism" by diasporic community. In his remarkable Wertheim lecture on long-distance nationalism in 1992, Anderson builds close links between capitalist order, mass migrations and mass communications. Reflecting upon the 'unaccountable nationalism' he concludes, "His political participation is directed towards an imagined *heimat* in which he does not intend to live, where he pays no taxes where he cannot be arrested, where he will not be brought before the courts—and where he does not vote: in effect a politics without responsibility or accountability" (11)

One major reason behind this diasporic engagement with homeland politically as argued by Lutz is, " the new racist nationalism which is gathering force in contemporary Europe is centrally concerned with the notions of defending home space and territory against 'the other', a category which has come to include immigrants, asylum seekers and ethnic minorities" (qtd.

Demers 88). This situation makes the position of diaspora an unstable one thereby forcing it to maintain close relationship with the homeland instead of putting everything at stake in a single nation. It explains why diaspora and international organizations work hand in hand having the rationale of Long Distance Nationalism at its base. Diasporic communities practising Long Distance Nationalism even to the extent of participating in the nationalist conflicts of their former homelands is particularly striking when they don't have any serious intention to return to their homelands. Demmers argues that the phenomenon of nationalism has in fact outgrown its definition. Contrary to the expectations of many, globalization hasn't meant the end of nationalism. Instead, nationalism has started to be carried out on a global scale. National communities have transcended borders and have become transnational national communities (93).

As outlined above, there are political, cultural, psychological and other valid reasons for diaspora to be practising long distance nationalism. Scholars have come to the consensus that its outcome has not always been positive in terms of global and communal harmony. The technological advancements via internet have in fact given wings to radical nationalism which aims at homogenization through violence. There is a huge upsurge in the radical nationalist organizations throughout the world in the name of virtual ethnic communities. Anderson's 'Imagined Communities' have really outgrown the traditional national-territorial borders with these virtual ethnic communities coming into existence. These internet based ethno-political communities can't be easily contained unless at the cost of curtailing fundamental human rights. The diasporic sentiment towards its homeland and its intention to belong to its home state have resulted in people with vested interest to utilize diaspora for their own personal radical ends. There are two crucial cases in this regard: non-state nationalist diaspora and state-related nationalist diaspora. The nationalist struggle for Tamil Eelam, Chechnya, Kashmir, belonging to the former category, are for political autonomy or reunification with the existing state. The expansion of *hindutva* project globally or the case of Chinese ultra-nationalists belong to the latter category of state related nationalist diaspora (Conversi 1358). Not to forget the global menacing forces of Islamic terrorism which resorts to nationalism in the name of Islamic Nation? Mary Kaldor writes: "In the late 1990s, a new variant of the new nationalism emerged with wholly new features. This was the ideology of Osama bin Laden and Al Qaeda. Of course, this is a religious movement but the ideologists of the nation talk about the 'Islamic Nation' and the basic idea of uniting around a common culture, Islam, and a religious language, Arabic, is a nationalist idea. It is a network, typical of global era. It is built up through new forms of communication, internet . . . satellite television . . . and new forms of violent struggle" (171). We all know how Islamic terrorism has grown exponentially and globally even after the killing of Osama bin Laden in 2011 by American military forces.

Much before internet arose on the global horizon, the pro-Khalistan movement led to the assassination of the then Prime Minister of India, Indira Gandhi by her Sikh bodyguards in November 1984 which was followed by anti-Sikh pogrom at the hands of activists from the ruling Congress party. Similarly, in the 21st century, Pro-hindutva organizations are on the rise with its major support base in Indian diaspora spread all across the world. There is an attempt by these extremist Hindu organizations to fill the communal pride of *hindutva* in the otherwise multicultural transnational diaspora. Diaspora politics has always entailed above average amount of radicalism with or without internet (Conversi 1372). The safety of being placed in another country, as scholars have argued, and the digital privacy guaranteed by anonymous world of internet add to the thrill, making diaspora even more indulgent in Long Distance

Nationalism. Globalization and internet revolution has strengthened diaspora so much that it now exercises clout in the policy-making of Nation States. Nevertheless, diaspora and internet alone are not entirely to be blamed for the radical nationalism of the present century. Nation states themselves promote patriotic chauvinism for their own political agenda. The lack of comprehensive cultural policies, lack of civic and cultural education, nation's promotion of patriotic chauvinism besides homogenizing effects of globalization, as outlined by Conversi, are some of the factors reinforcing radical nationalism in diaspora (1372). Besides, globalization should not be confused or equated with the development in digital communication and technology. Globalization is a much larger political, economic and cultural process which has benefitted from the digital revolution of the twenty-first century.

Globalization has played an instrumental role in the evolution of diaspora as a potent force to be reckoned with. Nationalism has become inter-territorial and transnational in character. More often than not we see Long Distance Nationalism of diaspora resulting in political conflicts often laden with violence. Contrary to the belief that multiculturalism and assimilation will lead to the demise of nationalism, it rather got a new lease of life on the wings of diaspora powered by globalization. No wonder long distance nationalism is often backed by the concerned Nation States in order to leverage diaspora for political mileage which undoubtedly makes nation states one of the biggest stake-holders in the process.

Work Cited

Anderson, Benedict. *Long-Distance Nationalism: World Capitalism and the Rise of Identity Politics*. Amsterdam, Centre for Asian Studies, 1992.

_____. *Imagined Communities: Reflections on the Origin and Spread of Nationalism.* London, Verso, 1991.

Hall, Stuart. "Cultural Identity and Diaspora." *Identity: Community, Culture, Difference*, ed. Jonathan Rutherford, Lawrence and Wishart, vol. 2, 1990.

Safran, William. "Diaspora in Modern Societies: Myth of Homeland and Return." *Diaspora: A Journal of Transnational Studies,* vol. 1, no. 1, 1991, pp. 83-99.

Conversi, Daniele. "Irresponsible Radicalization: Diaspora, Globalization and Long-Distance Nationalism in the Digital Age," *Journal of Ethnic and Migration Studies*. Routledge, vol. 38, 2012, pp. 1357-79.

Dufoix, Stéphane. "Diaspora and Nationalism," *Nations and Nationalism, A Global Historical Overview*, ed. Dave Kaplan and Guntram Herb, ABC-Clio, vol. 4, pp. 1364-78.

Kaldor, Mary. "Nationalism and Globalization," *Nations and Nationalism*, ASEN, vol. 10, 2004, pp. 161-77.

Schiller, Nina Glick. "Long Distance Nationalism," *Encyclopedia of Diasporas: Immigrant and Refugee Cultures around the World*, ed. Melvin Ember, Carol R. Ember, Ian Skoggard, Boston MA, Springer, 2005.

Demmers, Jolle. "Diaspora and Conflict: Locality, Long-Distance Nationalism, and Decolonization of Conflict Dynamics."*Javnost-The Public*, vol. 9, no. 1, 2002, pp. 85-96.

Clothing as an Important Part of Culture: Chitra Banerjee Divakaruni's "Clothes"

SWADHIKA P.
Res. Sch., Ethiraj College for Women, Chennai

Clothing is an important element of human civilization. It is often referred to as the social skin of human beings as it signifies our culture and society. Culture is significant in the identity formation and clothes are representation of the cultures. Clothing is a way of socializing the individuals into the society. It is an important element of identity to the diasporas. The short story "Clothes" written by Chitra Banerjee Divakaruni is from the collection *Arranged Marriage.* The author portrays the significance of clothes and its colours in the life of an immigrant woman.

Divakaruni is an expatriate writer. Her contribution is significant in portraying the experiences of diaspora women. The cause of migration is different for women from that of men. Men mostly migrate for higher economic opportunities, while migration for women is mainly effected by marriage. Women's experience of alienation is even more traumatic than men. They feel more insecure than men because of their economic dependence upon men. Divakaruni portrays the experiences and transitions of the protagonist Sumita in foreign land in this short story.

The transitions and multiple identities caused by marriage and migration in Diaspora women are significant in understanding their double consciousness of home and homelessness and they are often caught in between the cultures. Immigrant women who move after their marriage experience this in-between state in two ways, the first being taken away from their home to her in-law's place (immigration from mother's family to the groom's family) and the second shift is from their homeland to a foreign land. They experience double displacement in this migration.

The protagonist Sumita is a young, innocent girl from West Bengal. She gets married to Somesh who runs a store in the United States of America. Sumita moves to America soon after her wedding. She is happy with her husband but one night, he is shot dead at his workplace. Sumita becomes a young widow but develops the courage to run the store at the end of the story.

Divakaruni captures the emotional and psychological transformation of Sumita through her clothes. She portrays the different stages of the protagonist's life and transition in identity symbolically through the colours of the saris that she wears.

The description of the colours of the sari that the protagonist wears is unique to Indian culture and it also alludes to a culture-specific landscape or memory of the protagonist. The story begins with the description of Sumita bathing in the lake with her friends in a yellow sari. The protagonist compares her floating wet sari to a "sunflower after rain." This shows how the colour yellow is associated to the environment in which the protagonist has spent her early part of life.

In the description of the sari that Sumita wears when she meets Somesh's family she says: "It was the most expensive sari I had ever seen, and surely the most beautiful. Its body was a pale pink, like the dawn sky over the women's lake. The colour of transition." (1) In these lines she finds the colour to be indicative of her transition. She also compares it to the dawn sky over the lake. This is a culture-specific landscape in which she grew up. The sari also indicates the family wealth proving the social status of the father.

The colours are also associated with the beliefs and values of Sumita. Sumita associates colours to a particular value like the pale pink to that of a transitional colour, blue colour to be the colour of possibility and white to be the colour of ending.

The characters seem to be more particular about the colour as it is indicative of their life and identity. Sumita wishes to wear a blue colour sari for her travel in the plains because it would match the colour of the sky and her mother asks her to wear a red sari because she believes it to be colour of luck for the married woman. The narrator relates each colour to a specific memory of her motherland or a landscape or a culturally specific belief, this shows the nostalgia of the diaspora.

Sumita experiences cultural transformation through her migration to the United States. This transformation makes her develop double consciousness for the private (her house) and public (the outside world) realms. When she is at home with her in-laws, she wears saris but she wishes to wear western attires when she imagines herself moving out of her home for a job.

The transition in the identity of Sumita and her emotional state are also expressed through her clothes. Her transition from a maiden to a wife to a widow is expressed by her sari. After her husband's death she wears a white sari which is the colour of widowhood. The white sari symbolizes the emptiness of her life. She also calls it as the "colour of ending." The widowhood and the burden of it are expressed by the narrator only in terms of the clothes that she wears and its colours, emphasizing their significance in the character's consciousness. This proves that the emotions are expressed and experienced by culture-specific elements such as clothes and colours. In the description of the white sari she says: "There are waves and waves of white around my feet. I kick out in sudden rage, but the sari is too soft, it gives in too easily. I grab up an edge, clamp down with my teeth and pull, feeling a fierce, bitter satisfaction when I hear it rip." (5)

Sumita's admiration to the foreign culture is shown in her desire to wear western attires and speak the language. She feels a sense of pride when she understands and answers to the air-hostess in the flight. After Somesh's death she decides to run the store by herself and imagines herself in a skirt and blouse, the western attire that Somesh has bought her.

Works Cited

Agarwal, Beena. *Women Writers and Indian Diaspora.* Authorspress, 2011.

Divakaruni, Chitra Banerjee. "Clothes," *Arranged Marriage*. Penguin Random, 1995

Turner, Terence S. "The Social Skin," *HAU: Journal of Ethnography Theory*, 2 (2), 2012, pp. 486-504. HAUjournal, https://www.haujournal.org/.

Gender Inequalities in Sunetra Gupta's *So Good in Black*

MERCY THOMAS
Res. Sch., Stella Maris College (Autonomous), Chennai

Globalization with its magnetic promise of travel, lifestyle, and splendour unleashes fears and uncertainties among women. The theme "Women and Gender Issues" delves into the reality of gender problems faced by women in the globalized world with particular reference to Sunetra Gupta's novel *So Good in Black.* Gender attracts the attention of scholars all over the world; patriarchy and gender discourse are emerging disciplines. Women are exploited by men in different spheres, so the sense of gender had to emerge in the mind of feminist writers and activists throughout the world. Women were rarely the subjects of research and activities which are dominated by men. Feminist scholars sought to establish sex as biologically determined and gender as socially constructed. Women of all classes and castes have recognized the damaging violence against women as a major social issue. They are marginalized in economic, political, religious and cultural decision-making process. The women and children continue to go through deprivation, exploitation, and discrimination. According to Kamla Bhasin, gender issues are not women's issues alone as femininity does not exist in isolation from "masculinity." The image and power of one determines the image and power of the other. Damini was an educated, empowered woman, and an outstanding, fearless journalist. Her cousin Ela was a celebrity in dance, both in India and abroad. Their career and life made them victims of male domination, betrayal and sexism, reducing them into mere subordinates. Under the paternalistic dominance of Byron Mallick and her patriarchal husband, Ela could not bloom and develop her identity and the self-assured, independent and courageous Damini was murdered. Identity of an individual gets constructed through the interaction of various social aspects.

Judith Butler in *Gender Trouble* called for a new way of looking at sex and gender. She argues that gender should be seen as a fluid variable which shifts and changes in different contexts and at different times. She assessed gender as a social construction and body as a variable boundary that performs the cultural meanings of gender. "As soon as a child is born families and society begin the process of gendering. Birth of a son is celebrated, that of a daughter is mourned" (Vyas 21-22). Boys are encouraged to be tough and outgoing and girls are encouraged to be homebound and shy. These gender differences are created by the society. Gender inequality is distinct from other forms of economic and social inequalities. Gender inequality hampers the overall wellbeing of women, blocking them from participation in social, political, and economic activities, and can adversely affect the whole society (Vyas 57). Sexologist John Moncy coined the term gender role in 1955 and it is used to signify all those things that a person says or does to disclose himself or herself as having the status of boy or man, girl or woman, respectively (Arora 7).

"Byron Mallick never had a woman doubt his intelligence before, and realized with disappointment that being challenged by a woman is intolerable than being challenged by a man" (82). Challenging masculinity means challenging gender relations (Bhasin 55). Damini, the friend and cousin of Ela approached Byron to solve a problem in Coordinate Geometry and he could not provide a satisfactory answer. The impression and the mental picture he had about himself failed him. Byron Mallick seemed to have believed that he has the right answers to every problem.

In front of Damini and Ela he felt miserable because he was challenged by the girls whom he considered inferior to him. Gender differences result from socialization. Society establishes a set of cultural expectations for each gender and children are taught to conform to what society expects. He lacked the nobility to accept himself as he is. His attitude and behaviour traits are socially prescribed, taught, and learned; that a man should never be inferior in front of a woman. He failed to value the girls and their worth, and his behaviour can be described as a hegemonic masculinity. Judith Butler argues that all gendered behaviour is a matter of the internalization of social expectations (57).

Ann Oakley, the feminist scholar, says, "Gender is a matter of culture, it refers to the social classification of men and women into 'masculine' and 'feminine.' Gender has no biological origin, that the connection between sex and gender are not really 'natural' at all" (Bhasin 2). Many use the term sex and gender to mean the same thing, but there is a difference between them. The term sex refers to the biological distinction of being male or female whereas the term gender refers to the social or learned characteristics that are associated with being male or female. Gender is the result of socio-cultural influences throughout an individual's development. Boys are moulded to become what society considers to be masculine: assertive and independent; girls what society considers to be feminine: caring and dependable. Behaviours which match these expectations are rewarded while behaviours that violate these expectations are often associated with costs (Schneider 331)

Research by Condry and Condry found that when a male child cries, people will say that he is angry. When a female child cries, they say she is frightened. This process continues as the individual grows into adulthood. This way of describing is done by men and women across the country according to a study made by Williams and Best in 1982. Man for example is more frequently associated with descriptors such as aggressive, capable, and rational whereas women are affectionate, caring, and emotional (Schneider 331). According to Judith Butler gender is an act or a sequence of acts that is always and inevitably occurring since it is impossible to exist as a social agent outside the terms of gender (Eagleton 47). "Gender operates as a set of hierarchically arranged roles in modern society, masculine and feminine. The binary division of gender can take several forms. The two halves seem to be equal but opposite in a complementary relationship. Often the two halves will be typified as opposite and with the female in the inferior position" (Francis 2).

Byron Mallick noticed that after the summer vacation with her cousin Damini, Ela had transformed and used terms like 'comprador' and 'bourgeoisie' and found in them both Marxist tendencies. They did not respect Byron's words and questioned his motives and challenged his attitude towards human rights. There was a crisis of confidence between them and he was ignored. He did not get the usual welcome from her after his return from a business trip. The situation was very tedious and distressing for him and Damini appeared to be a threat to his ideology. According to him her orphanage was only an object of pity, charity, welfare, and was just dispensable. "Gender assignment is established and maintained by people in authority operating in an official capacity for the state" (Brush 43). Patriarchy is the cause of gender inequalities, subordination, and other discriminations against women.

Byron did not like to see Ela and Damini together in his house. After a heated discussion on protectionism between the three, Ela rushed out to the boarding house without even saying good bye to Byron. His immediate response was to inform her father. He felt upset and humiliated by this event. He failed to understand that Damini and Ela did not like to be controlled and resent anything which curtails their freedom. They needed friends who are supportive, authentic, and accessible, and who would empower them. Damini and Ela found Byron incoherent, unauthentic as he was too authoritative in his ways. Patriarchy finds various ways to exercise their authority over women and children. They feel responsible for everything and Byron has been playing the role of a patriarch. The conflict between Mallick and Damini arose because the ideologies of both differed. According to Kamla Bhasin, the emphasis on economic growth, pursuit of profit, and individualism, widened the gap between men and women, rich and poor, north and south. Men need to undergo a major change of values from self-assertion and competition to co-operation, and social justice, from expansion to conservation, from material acquisition to inner growth (49-50).

Byron Mallick focused on profit in his business and Damini on humanitarian service for the poor and marginalized women. Damini was not encouraged to occupy the public space which was her passion and right as a citizen of the country. Instead she was threatened and prevented from carrying on freely with her choice. She had the right to be part of her community and exercise her freedom publicly but it was viewed and treated differently. She did the right thing by choosing to serve the marginalized according to her perception. Byron could have solved the conflict, by treating her as an equal. Masculinity hinders women from progressing and stands as a barrier to their development. According to Bauman, the modern world in which people live is one, whose very value leads, not to understanding and toleration, but to authoritarianism and the systematic elimination of difference (Evans 2).

Damini was an independent thinker and her influence on Ela was not acceptable to Byron. He did not develop Ela's critical thinking because she was a girl, she was overprotected and was hindered from thinking for herself. He expected them to play only the role assigned by the family and society. Women are kept dominated and subordinated by most of the masculine world. "Gender relations are relations of dominance and subordination with elements of co-operation, force, and violence sustaining them (Bhasin 2000: 27). Gender differences result from socialization. Society establishes a set of cultural expectations for each gender and children are taught to conform to what society expects. "Gender-based occupational segregation is one of the most important factors contributing to inequality between men and women in labour markets around the world (Loutfi 9). Mallick did not realize that women can influence the society and can affect matters of their lives, the families, and the communities connected to them. Women see other's struggle as their own struggles and live in solidarity with them. They experience gender oppressions to a great extent due to the patriarchal domination of the society. Everything regarding women is seen as feminine and is undervalued. "Problems arise when patriarchy imposes one set of qualities on men and another on women. It is this imposition of stereotyped qualities which leads to the creation of domineering, intolerant, aggressive men, and subservient, spineless, fearful women. To develop their potential, both boys and girls, men and women should imbibc positive "masculine" and positive "Feminine" qualities (Bhasin 1986: 28).

As a social construct, gender refers to norms, values, customs, and practices by which biological differences are transformed, and exaggerated into a much wider social system (Bhasin 6). From the time a girl is born, she is treated according to the gender assignment, and learns to adopt gender appropriate behaviours. At times patriarchy appears to be irrelevant with regard to names, dress code, games, rewards, punishments, the attention given, the subjects offered for study, the jobs assigned and so on. Everyone is shaped by gender expectations and females suffer most due to the rigid gender roles. Women are seen as incapable of intelligent decisions. Butler declares that Gender is by definition 'unnatural,' so that there is no necessary relationship between one's body and one's gender (1990: 35). She departs from the common assumption that sex, gender, and sexuality exist in relation to each other. One may be a 'masculine' female or a 'feminine' male. She argues that 'sex by definition, will be shown to have been gender all along' (1990: 8). In literary studies, the term specifically refers to how individuals define themselves and how they are evaluated by others on the basis of gender. Gender is often associated with feminism. Gender is also the study of power relationships, how one's gender gives one a power advantage over the other gender. Gender roles are the codes of behaviour that a society expects from one gender or another (Vyas 21).

The training Ela received with the aid of Byron turned her into a professional dancer and the national and international dance programmes she performed made her a renowned celebrity. Under the hegemonic power, her will is subjugated and aspirations controlled. The marriage for her was a transition from an independent and happy life to restrictions, norms, and patriarchal rules. Arjun colonized her mind with his friendship, phone calls, promises, and succeeded to get her as his wife and confined her to his home and never made an attempt to understand her inner longing and desires, and to treat her with equality. She was never a threat to him in continuing the various aspects of patriarchy. "In patriarchy, gender is a category that functions to establish and reinforce inequality. The gender roles are rigid, repressive, and reactionary. These roles constrain the healthy flourishing of both males and females, but females experience by far the most significant psychological and physical injuries from the system." (Jansen). Gender based prejudices and divisions in many societies mainly affect girls and women and it is based on the views that they are physically and emotionally weak and inferior, in comparison to men and boys, dependent, subordinate, and a burden to family (Enarson and Chakrabarty 7).

Gender is not a process, but it is a particular type of process, a set of repeated acts within a highly rigid regulatory frame as Butler puts it (63). According to Butler gender is an act or a sequence of acts that is always and inevitably occurring, since it is impossible to exist as a social agent outside the terms of gender (47). *Gender Trouble* of Judith Butler argues that gender is acquired rather than given, that women and men have elaborate expectations of femininity and masculinity and that gender is crucial to social cohesion and social order (58). Parents teach gender norms through non-conscious, routine forms of interaction, rewarding behaviour that are gender/ sex appropriate discouraging those that are not. They believe that girls who adopt traditional masculine behaviour will raise their social status, but boys who adopt feminine behaviour risk their social status (DeFrancisco et al 161).

Gerda Lerner states, "Men and women live on a stage, on which they act out their assigned roles, equal in importance. The play cannot go on without both kinds of performers. Neither of them "contributes" more or less to the whole; neither marginal nor dispensable. But the stage set, is conceived, painted, and defined by men. Men have written the play, have directed the show, interpret the meanings of action. They have assigned themselves the most interesting, most heroic parts, giving women the supporting roles. It is not that women are absolutely excluded from power or prestige in patriarchy--the problem is with the framework itself, and the framework is determined by men (Bhasin, "What is Patriarchy?" 15). Like states and social policies gender is about power. Through gender relations people continually recreate and reinforce the distinction between masculinity and feminity. It is also about drawing a clear, bright line between men and women (Butler 11).

In the gender context, Ela's position is that of a slave. Arjun claims to be the 'subject' and Ela comes under the category of the 'other.' She could not think independently or decide for herself, but carry out the tradition of taking care of the household duties, an unpaid labour. In fact she has been playing the role of a shadow of Arjun and when the shadow left for his business to distant places, her suppressed feelings and cravings, and the unfulfilled desires emerged out. She enjoyed a sort of freedom in the absence of her dominant patriarchal husband and befriended Max. Patriarchy did not respect women and Arjun made no effort to understand and listen to the subaltern Ela. Ashley Brilliant, a popular writer, quips, "It is difficult to communicate on a moving planet." Arjun's busy schedules and hectic business ignored the voice of his adorable wife. She had a voice within, but could not articulate with her husband who was a workaholic. There was an element of noise which is caused by cultural, social and economic factors, and the subaltern could not be heard. Pierce O'Reilly observes that the parting of Arjun Mitra for a long business trip was just casual and he remarked that there was an absence of emotion between the couples. The subaltern can't speak because their words cannot be properly interpreted though it is not a failure of articulation. Arjun does not make any conscious effort to listen to her as he is busy with his business. The empowered Ela before her marriage, is disempowered in her new surrounding in the patriarchal family of Arjun.

"A little chalk in milk will not kill anyone," Byron says to Max. "Better surely for them to drink something resembling milk than no milk at all" (4). Byron justifies his action of sending adulterated milk to Damini's shelter home. "Masculinity is always local and subject to change. What does not change," says Arthur Brittain, "is the justification and naturalization of male power, or masculine ideology." Justifying one's wrong doing is as old as civilization itself. Though Byron was a friend of Damini, he did not like to be confronted by her, but wanted to silence her by causing her murder as he found himself helpless in front of the fearless journalist Damini. She was committed to communicating the truth and this attitude of Damini was a challenge to him and the reputation he built up would be completely destroyed. It was difficult for him to part with his popularity and friends. Masculinity always maintained power, status, or influence during challenging times by all means" (Carrel 501).

In most social relations men are subjects; their desires, likes and dislikes, and their satisfactions are paramount. Kamla Bhasin says, women at best are junior and passive partners, at worst, commodities, intended to satisfy men's desires or lust (2004: 29). 'Gender is the linguistic index of the political opposition between the sexes. Gender is used in the singular as there are no two genders. There is only one: the feminine, the "masculine" not being a gender. For the masculine is not the masculine, but the general.' Hence Wittig calls for the destruction of "sex" so that women can assume the status of a universal subject. On the way toward that destruction, "women must assume both a particular and a universal point of view" (Butler 20). Sex is a war in the minds of men, for those women who refuse to respond or submit to sexual advances sometimes face horrible consequences. Sometimes men throw acid on women who reject them, even kill them saying, "If I can't have her, nobody else will"; or rape them saying, "No one say no to me" (Bhasin 31). Male sexual violence is widespread everywhere and its threat makes it impossible for women to enter public spaces. Violent male sexuality is responsible for the sexual harassment taking place in public places like the streets, buses, schools and colleges.

Women's groups have organized gender awareness workshops and trainings to enable women to become activists, and initiate the process of women's empowerment in order to achieve gender equality. Women's Studies has emerged as a strong and multidisciplinary approach to analyzing gender issues. Debates on equality aimed at changing the roles, attitudes and status of women brought about some changes. Kamla Bhasin argues that challenging masculinity means challenging gender relations (55). Mallick felt horribly smug when he could not solve the problem in Coordinate Geometry for Damini. The impression and the mental picture he had about himself failed him. He felt miserable because the girls whom he considered inferior to him challenged his knowledge. Patriarchal men always seek success, power and positions. Mallick failed to value the girls and their worth, and his behaviour can be described as masculine dominance. Men criticize and ridicule feminists and feminism because of their own discomfort with feminism. Sometime the discomfort is expressed as jokes, fear, and sometimes as an outright attack on feminists. Some of the gender-based problems that women face are limitations in mobility, social restrictions and accompaniment by mates, greater risk of sexual and domestic violence, sexual abuse, low education, socially assigned roles like caring for children, elderly and sick.

Work Cited

Arora, Premalatha, *Women, Gender and Modern Society*. Pacific, 2011.

Bhasin, Kamla. *Exploring Masculinity*. Kali for Women, 2004.

_____. *Feminism and its Relevance in South Asia*. Women Unlimited, 1986.

_____. *Understanding Gender*. Kali for Women, New Delhi, 2000.

Brush, Lisa D. *Gender and Governance*. Rawat, 2007.

Butler, Judith .*Gender and Governance*. Rawat, 2007.

_____. *Gender Trouble: Feminism and the Subversion of Identity*. Routledge, 1990.

Carrel, Michael R., et al. *Fundamentals of Organizational Behaviour*. Prentice Hall, 1997.

DeFrancisco, Victoria Pruin and Catherine Helen Palezewski. *Communicating Gender Diversity: A Critical Approach*. Sage, London, 2007.

Eagleton, Mary. *Feminist Literary Theory: A Reader*. Wiley Blackwell, 2011.

Enarson, Elaine and P.G. Dhar Chakrabarty. *Women, Gender and Disaster: Global Issues and Initiatives*. Sage, New Delhi, 2009.

Evans, Mary. *Gender and Social Theory*. Rawat, 2009.

Francis, Anne Cranny. *Gender Issues: Terms and Debates*. Palgrave Macmillan, 2003.

Jansen, Robert. Dgrnewsservice.org/civli/pat/gender/basic-propositions -sex-gender-patriarchy.

Loutfi, Martha Fetherolf. *Women, Gender and Work: What is equality and how do we get there?* Rawat, New Delhi, 2002.

Salih, Sara. *Judith Butler.* Routledge, New York, 2002.

Schneider, Frank W. *Applied Social Psychology: Understand and Addressing Social and Practical Problems*. Sage, 2012.

Vyas, Ashutosh. *Gender Issues and Women Empowerment, Dimensions and Development*. Book Enclave, 2016 (21).

The Problem of Displacement in Bharati Mukherjee's *The Tiger's Daughter*

T. ABIRAMI and P. KIRUTHIKA
Res. Sch., Periyar University P.G. Ext. Centre, Dharmapuri

The last few decades have witnessed a remarkable change in the perspective of women in Indian English fiction. As a natural consequence, their writings reflect what we consider an expatriate sensibility generated due to the cultural disparity and emotional disintegration. In the process it is the woman who suffers the most because of her multiple dislocations; as a result their writing expresses the stereotypical sufferings of woman.

Bharati Mukherjee depicts women, their different relationships, the dominance of patriarchal practices in traditional society, as also the forms of liberation and empowerment which are available to women in the Diaspora situation.

The novel *The Tiger's Daughter* gives a fine manifestation of cultural conflict. It is an interesting story of an upper class Bengali Brahmin girl, Tara Banerjee who goes to America for higher studies. Though afraid of the unknown ways of America, she marries an American. She returns to India after seven years, only to find herself a total stranger in the inherited milieu. She then realizes that she is now neither Indian nor American.

The starting point of the story is a rainy night in the year 1879. It was the day of the grand wedding ceremony of the daughters of Hari Lal Banerjee, the 'Zamindar.' In the village Pachapara, there standing under a wedding canopy on the roof of his house, Hari Lak Banerjee could have hardly imagined what future holds in store for his coming generations. He "did not hear the straining and imprisoned ghost of change" (2). This is so because "the shadows of suicide or exile, of Bengali soil sectioned and ceded; of workers rising against their bosses could not have been divined by even a wise man in those days" (6). After the marriage of Hari Lal Banerjee's daughters, life continued to be pleasant in the village. After two summers, Hari Lal Banerjee falls a prey to an unseen assassin while mediating a feud. All the reputation and influence of Banerjee family died with him. Years later a young woman who had never been to Pachapara would grieve for the Banerjee family and try to analyze the reasons for its change. "She would sit by a window in America to dream of Hari Lal, Her great-grandfather, and she would wonder at the gulf that separated him from herself." (9)

This young woman is nobody else but Tara Banerjee, the great-granddaughter of Hari Lal Banerjee and Thomas (Tobacco) Corporation Limited. Tara is packed off by her father at the early age of fifteen for America for higher studies. In Poughkeepsie, she feels homesick. As it is typical of Indians who are proud of their family and genealogy, she defends her family and her country instinctively. At such moments when she thinks like breaking, she even prays to goddess Kali for strength. In the beginning she could not adjust to the culture of the United States because of her deep-rooted Indianness. In India, a marriage is not simply a union of two individuals; it is a coming together of two families as well. But in Western countries, marriage is simply a contract between two individuals. As ill-luck would have it, Tara falls in love with an American named David and marries him. David is totally western and Tara finds it difficult to communicate the finer nuances of her family background and of her life in Calcutta because of the cultural differences. "Her husband asked questions about Indian customs and traditions. She felt insecure in an alien atmosphere. Madison square was unbearable and her husband was after all a foreigner" (50).

In spite of her Americanized personality, the Indian pulse vibrating in Tara makes her realize that the life in Calcutta, in spite of all the dark spots and drawbacks, has its unique features, not found anywhere else and which her husband David is unable to recognize. Tara has no more an Indian identity and is always in clash with the culture of her native soil. The clash is deeply felt in the psyche of Tara who finds it difficult to adjust with the traditions of her own family. At the Bombay airport, she responds to her relatives in a cold and dispassionate manner.

The railway station looks like a hospital with so many sick and deformed men sitting on the bundles and trunks. In the compartment she finds it difficult to travel with a Marwari and a Nepali. Now she considers America a dreamland. Her mind resists the changed atmosphere in her native place. Slowly her changed personality makes her a misfit in the company of her old friends. She feels alienated when her relatives call her, 'Americawali' and her husband 'Mleccha.' The foreignness of her spirit refuses to establish an emotional kinship with her old friends and relatives. The greatest irony of her return is that she feels lonely in her native land. Tara's mother is a saintly woman and she spends a great deal of time in her prayer room. At home, Tara is compelled to lead a pious life. Her mother urges her to sit and listen to Sanskrit shlokas, but she tries to tolerate prayers. After her return from America, she finds it difficult to sing the song "Raghupati Raghava Raja Ram."

Caught in the gulf between the two contrasting worlds—India and America, Tara regrets that she has forgotten many of the Hindu rituals of worshipping icons she had seen her mother performing since her childhood. American culture has covered Tara like an invisible spirit. In the deepest core of her heart, she has an intense desire to behave like an ordinary Indian. She realizes that she has become rootless now. She sees everything with an American eye and comments on everything from the point of view of an Americanized Indian. She finds herself marginalized on the psychological level and suffers from a split self.

She hopes that her friends would offer peace to her confused state. To her surprise, they behave in a different way. The novelist, through Tara, calls them "racial pursuits" (86). When Tara writes to David regularly she fails to communicate her feelings and failures in her homeland. Tara becomes confused for she cannot share her feelings with her American husband. She remains a foreigner to both her husband and her friends.

She finds it difficult to relate to her family, city, culture in general since her marriage to an American and her western education are enough signs to brand her as an alienated westernized woman. The implicit logic is that since she is exposed to the west and has absorbed its values she must be necessarily alienated. Tara is able to understand the changes in her personality due to her total Americanization. Inspired by her Westernization, she cannot face the disease, despair and poverty of people in Calcutta. There occurs a conflict in her mind between her old senses of perception and her present changed outlook. Jasbir Jain observes in this connection: "Tara's consciousness of the present is rooted in her life in the States and when she looks at India anew it is not through the eyes of her foreign husband David. Her reactions are those of a tourist, of a foreigner." (13)

Tara's stay in the States has changed her view and vision of India. It has opened her eyes to the gulf between the lives of the poor and those of the rich in her own country. Being a westernized Indian she looks at India as a land of the poor living in a poor environment and suffering from starvation and disease. Tara cherished memories of the greenery and forests of her childhood but these are not to be found anymore. Tara herself has changed due to the years she has spent in the west. She hardly has a feeling of being 'at home' in her homeland. Tara is torn between her feelings for home and exile. Sometimes she feels like going back to her husband David where she may be more at ease. Tara regrets that she has forgotten many Hindu rituals of worshipping: "She could not remember the next step of the ritual. It was not a simple loss. Tara feared, this forgetting of prescribed, it was a little death, a hardening of the heart, a cracking of axis and centre." (51) A sense of displacement always works within the heart of a diasporan.

Tara feels bored, shocked and to some extent even stunned with her friends in Calcutta. She can feel an implicit malice in them. Her marriage only makes her embarrassed among her friends and relatives at home. Whereas marriage is a means of assimilation for a Diasporic individual abroad, at home it hangs on her heart as a 'burden' (62). Though Tara's culture and David's culture are not same, Tara tries to build up a harmonious matrimonial relationship by keeping her home and exile in two separate compartments.

To entertain her, her friends take her to a trip to Darjeeling to spend her summer. But Tara gets no consolation and peace. She becomes upset when a heart-specialist passes sarcastic remarks on her: "I think your years abroad have robbed you of your feminine propriety" (187). Unable to reconcile with the situation, Tara feels like going back to America. At Nayapur, when she meets a Marwari named Tuntunwala, it leads to her rape by this wicked man. But Tara hides this incident of seduction from others for fear of disgrace. She could not share her knowledge of Tuntunwala with any of her friends. "In a land where a friendly smile, and accidental brush of fingers, can ignite rumors--even lawsuits--how is one to speak of Mr. Tuntunwala's violence" (199). Here, because of her acculturation, Tara looks down upon Indian culture, as a typical westerner. She is unhappy about the conservative culture of India in which she was brought up as an orthodox girl in a disciplined rural environment.

In New York, she had dreamt of coming back to Calcutta, but "the return had brought only wounds" (25). Tara yearns to go back to David. She goes to Air India office and reserves a ticket to New York. Her journey is decided but after a short time of this reservation Tara becomes a victim of violence. Indeed, at the novel's end, Tara discovers that after seven years of being away, she had "slipped outside" the safe space of home to which she had thought she belonged, and that "re-entry was barred" (110). The novel ends on the final symbolic image of Tara suspended in a state of terror and uncertainty. Locked in a car outside the Catelli-Continental Hotel, she is surrounded by a violent mob of Naxalite protesters who have just attacked the old aristocrat, Joyonto, and killed her friend, the businessman Pronob. As the narrative comes to a close, Tara's last thoughts are about whether "she would ever get out of Calcutta" (210).

Mukherjee's life is a story of exile, expatriation and dispossession that constitute her unique Diasporic consciousness which is responsible for her creative expression. Her writings reflect her personal experience in cross-cultural encounter. Mukherjee's protagonist Tara suffers from the cultural turmoil as the novelist herself suffered in real life. It seems that the novelist projects herself through the character of Tara, a victim of split personality and identity crisis.

The Tiger's Daughter reflects the confrontation between illusion and reality. It adopts the technique of documentation to bring out the contrast between two worlds and two attitudes. The gulf between the world of western liberation represented by Tara and David and conservatism and Indianness represented by her mother cannot be bridged and Tara's psyche remains split up like other immigrants.

Thus, in *The Tiger's Daughter* Mukherjee shows that the native nation as the place of ultimate refuge and gratification is a myth and the immigrant can never return to it. Tara's quest for self proves frustrating leading her to disillusion, depression and alienation and finally ending in a tragedy. The greatest irony of the novel is that Tara survives the racial hardships in a foreign country but becomes a victim in her native soil--her home, where she had come to seek peace.

Works Cited

Mukherjee, Bharati. *The Tiger's Daughter.* New Delhi: Penguin, 1990.

Brady, Veronica. "Straddling Two Cultures with reference of *The Tiger's Daughter*," *CRNLE Reviews Journal*, 1. 2 (1998).

Bradley, C. Edwards, ed. *Conversations with Bharati Mukherjee*. University Press of Mississippi, 2005.

Eliot, T.S. "Tradition and Individual Talent." *20th Century Literary Criticism*, ed. David Lodge. London: Routledge: Kegan Paul, 1996.

Jain, Jasbir. "Foreignness of Spirit: The World of Bharati Mukherjee's Novels," *The Journal of Indian Writing in English*, 13.2: (1985): 12-19

Iyengar, Srinivasa K.R. *Indian Writing in English.* New Delhi: Sterling, 1985.

Cultural Crisis in Jhumpa Lahiri's "Interpreter of Maladies" and "Sexy"

V. SRILATHA
Stanley College of Engg. & Tech. for Women, Hyderabad

Jhumpa Lahiri, the well-known short story writer, is winner of the Pulitzer Prize for her first collection of short stories *Interpreter of Maladies*. She narrates the lives of Indians in exile through her elegant stories. The characters navigate between their inherited tradition and the baffling situations they encounter in the new world. The present paper deals with two stories "Interpreter of Maladics" and "Sexy," focusing on the cultural crisis of the characters who stumble upon inexplicable situations in the society and assert themselves finally.

Mr. Kapasi, the protagonist in 'Interpreter of Maladies' is a forty-six-year old person who works as a tourist guide on Fridays and Saturdays. He guides Mr. and Mrs. Das, who visit India from America. He takes them to various tourist spots like Sun Temple and hills of Udayagiri and Khandagiri. As they continue their journey, Mr. Kapasi has conversation with Mr. Das, who reveals that he and his wife Mina were born and brought up in America and their parents are from India. As the conversation goes on, Mr. Das asks Mr. Kapasi about his job. Mr. Kapasi reveals that he works in a doctor's office as an interpreter. As Das couple expresses their curiosity regarding his job, he explains that he interprets the maladies of Gujarati patients to the doctor who does not know the language.

Listening to their conversation, Mrs. Das says dreamily that "it's romantic" but appreciates that his job has great responsibility. She requests him to tell more about his job by offering a piece of gum. Mr. Kapasi is surprised with the words of Mrs. Das and shares with the couple his experience as an interpreter to patients. He also recalls that he "had been a devoted scholar of foreign languages; the owner of an impressive collection of dictionaries." He has dreamt of becoming an interpreter of diplomats and dignitaries, resolving the conflicts and settling the disputes between the two parties. He thinks that his job of interpretation is a sign of his failings. When his first son had contracted typhoid, at the age of seven, it was difficult for him to pay the medical bills. When the doctor offered him to pay double the amount he earned as an English teacher at a grammar school, he accepted the job to pay his son's medical bill. Later, his son died of burning fever; he could not console his wife who spent many sleepless nights. She has no respect for his job as it reminds her of their dead son. Mr. Kapasi, whose job nobody appreciated, is fascinated with the words of Mrs. Das and tries to express his love for her but encounters a baffling situation.

Mrs. Das understands that Mr. Kapasi interprets maladies of different patients and helps them in getting rid of their ailments. So, she feels inclined to disclose the fact of her distress to Mr. Kapasi. When Mr. Kapasi compliments Bobby, the youngest son of the couple, "A brave little boy," she opens up saying that it is not so surprising and reveals that the little boy, Bobby, is not the son of Raj, her husband.

She discloses that they studied in the same school and Raj proposed her during their school days. When they realized that they could not live separate even for a minute, they joined the same college and got married. After their marriage they had two children Tina and Ronny and being busy with the motherhood she could not maintain her friendship with others for a long time. She recalls how she wanted to be with Raj her entire life. Raj and Mina's parents were friends and spent time together during weekends. They used to send Raj and Mina upstairs to play, enjoyed their tea downstairs, joking about their marriage. She reveals the secrets of the time spent with Raj which reflects her love and affection for him.

She reveals that once Raj had told that his Punjabi friend, whom she has met once but may not remember, is coming to their home to stay for a week to attend an interview. The Punjabi friend makes love with her in Raj's absence in a smart way. Bobby is his son and this guilt haunts her. She regrets that she was not loyal to her husband. As Beauvoir says it is "unjust and immoral to use the sexual difference to exploit women" (Shukla 155) like this. In frustration, she feels like throwing everything through the window. She cannot bear the memory of the unpleasant incident. She could not confess it to Raj or disclose it to anyone. She reveals it to Mr. Kapasi, who is an interpreter, with the hope that he would suggest some remedy to get rid of the guilty feeling she has been carrying for the past eight years.

Mr. Kapasi as an interpreter of maladies has observed many patients and has studied their psychology. He has never come across a person like Mrs. Das. "She did not resemble the patients in the doctor's office, those who came glassy eyed and desperate, unable to sleep or breathe." From his point of view, she has been suffering from the guilt due to cultural differences for the past eight years. "For eight years I haven't been able to express this to anybody, not to friends, certainly not to Raj. He doesn't even suspect it. He thinks I'm still in love with him."

Mr. Kapasi, who has felt infatuated with her beauty, is shocked when she confesses. He feels depressed and realizes later that Mrs. Das considers him a doctor. He decides to suggest her to convey the thing to Mr. Das as honesty is the best policy. He wants to settle the issue as a mediator interpreting the situation, to get rid of her pain as per her request. He understands the sensitivity of Mrs. Das and decides to give her comfort by safeguarding her from monkeys without revealing about the trail of monkeys following her to attack her.

As the story unfolds, Bobby the boy suddenly seems to be missing. Actually, the boy has been surrounded by a group of monkeys. As everyone comes to rescue the boy, Mrs. Das's mood shifts from the painful thought to love towards her son. She requests Mr. Das that they should leave the place immediately and he accepts. Mr. Kapasi starts the car, takes them away from the place and drops them at their destination. He observes and retains the picture of the Das family and leads a normal life.

Similarly, Miranda, the protagonist in the story "Sexy" feels entangled in the love affair of Dev, Devajit Mitra, a married man from Bengal who works in an investment bank, and endures the situation. Miranda works for a public radio station in the fund-raising department. She works along with Laxmi, who sits in the next cubicle in the same department. The story deals with Laxmi's conversations about her cousin's life, and Miranda's observation and comparison of her life with Dev.

The story begins with the conversation of Laxmi with Miranda about her cousin's nightmare at their workplace. Laxmi often converses on phone with her husband or cousin. Her frequent conversations on phone distract Miranda. She conveys that her cousin's husband after nine years of their marriage has fallen in love with another woman who sat next to him on a plane.

When Laxmi says that her cousin's husband knows four languages as he was brought up by a Punjabi mother and Bengali father and has learnt French and English at school, Miranda thinks that Dev is a Bengali.

As the story unfolds, Miranda is being brought up along with Dixit's family at Michigan. She was timid at the age of nine. "Miranda . . . had been too frightened even to walk on the same side of the street as the Dixit house . . . even held her breath until she reached the next lawn" and at the age of nineteen she started dating her school and college boys. When she met Dev for the first time at Filene in a shopping complex, she was fascinated with his physical appearance and thought that she should not miss that man. "Miranda didn't know what she wanted. All she knew was that she didn't want the man to walk away." She feels that the man is "lingering, waiting" along with the saleswoman to tell something to Miranda.

When Miranda interacts with Dev, she understands that Dev has shopped for his wife who is going to India for a few weeks. Her infatuation makes her feel that being with Dev "didn't seem so wrong" without the wife. Miranda and Dev spend time every night together almost, she watches every move of Dev and admires him. She feels that Dev was the first person to admire her unlike the other boys she dated in the college. "Dev was the first always to pay for things and hold doors open and reach across a table in a restaurant to kiss her hand . . . the first to whisper her name again and again when they made love."

She builds an attachment with Dev and wants to put her photograph with Dev in her cubicle at the office similar to the photo which Laxmi has kept in her cubicle; the photo of Laxmi and her husband which they have taken at Taj Mahal. On the other hand, Dev gives priority to his family. He leaves Miranda in the middle of the night and goes to his house to attend his wife's call at 6 o'clock in the morning every day. When Laxmi argues with her husband on phone in a conversation, Miranda feels that Dev never argued with her and she recalls how they enjoyed going to movies and restaurants.

When Dev goes to airport to receive his wife who has just returned from India, Miranda goes to Filene's basement and buys all the things which a mistress needs and dreams of meeting Dev the next Sunday. During the week she recalls the time she spent with Dev and waits for him.

At office, Laxmi vents her emotions talking about her cousin's husband who asks for divorce. Marriage is "an organized rape" (Pandey 11). She says it hasn't been for the first time that he has had affair with other women; and her cousin bears him just for the sake of boy, "if I were her, I'd fly straight to

London and shoot them both. . . . I don't know how she can just wait this way." Miranda feels that she knows how to wait for Dev.

When Dev visits the next Sunday, Miranda asks him about the looks of his wife hesitantly and wonders "if they'd quarrel." Dev is not surprised by the question and says that his wife resembles Madhuri Dixit, the actress from Bombay. Miranda feels shocked and her "heart stopped" instantly. Unlike her expectations, Dev doesn't admire her but he just makes love with her.

Miranda meets Laxmi's cousin, who comes to visit Laxmi at her workplace. Laxmi in order to console her cousin requests Miranda to bear with the little boy Rohin, the son of Laxmi's cousin. When Miranda spends time with Rohin, she realizes the pain of his mother. She recalls Dev and is disturbed. She cries and thinks: "it is much more important to be oneself than anything else" (Woolf 109). She asserts herself finally and decides to avoid Dev to lead a normal life.

Thus, in the story "Interpreter of Maladies," Mr. Kapasi overcomes his infatuation with Mrs. Das; Mrs. Das endures the pain of cultural crisis for eight long years and settles down with her husband. Again, in the story "Sexy," Miranda gives up the thought of making love with Dev, a married man. The protagonists in both the stories understand the situation and decide to lead a normal life.

Works Cited

Lahiri, Jhumpa. *Interpreter of Maladies*. India: Harper Collins, 2017.

Pandey, Miti. *Feminism in Contemporary British and Indian English Fiction*. New Delhi: Sarup, 2003.

Shukla, B.A. *The French Feminists and "The Second Sex."* Jaipur: Book Enclave, 2008.

Woolf, Virginia. *A Room of One's Own*. Australia: Penguin, 2003.

Witnessing the Revolution: *Feda'i* as a Storyteller

ISHRAT BASHIR
Central University of Kashmir

War and violence have become ubiquitous in our world today. Story-telling could be a form of resistance to the chaos engendered by violence whether in the name of justice or freedom from oppression. Elias Khoury, an eminent novelist from Lebanon, weaves his stories in the substratum of the civil war of Lebanon and uses a *feda'i* (a fighter) as the narrator attempting to narrate the unnarratable from within the war. The present paper attempts to analyze how Khoury's *feda'i* the narrator evolves from a fighter to a witness and story-teller. The *feda'i* fights in the war but at the same time tells the story of it as it is unfolding, laying bare all its contradictions and disillusionment. In the process, the capacity for self-criticism emerges as a composite element of any revolutionary consciousness.

Feda'i (militant) is a significant structural and functional element in most of Elias Khoury's fiction. Khoury had been actively involved in the student activism at Lebanese University in the 1960s. After the Arab-Israeli war of 1967 in which Arabs were defeated, many Palestinians from West Bank fled to Jordan and other neighbouring countries. A group of Christian students including Khoury himself visited a Palestinian refugee camp at Baqa'a in Jordan. Khoury found the conditions in the camp "unspeakable, enough to make you weep" (Interview).

Though he had always supported Palestinians' right to their own land from which they were ousted, he decided to join their struggle more actively. After he returned to Beirut, he joined Fatah. Fatah, formerly called Palestinian National Liberation Movement, is a Palestinian nationalist political organization that trained many militant groups to fight against Israel. Khoury was also trained as a militant (*feda'i*) and worked in South Lebanon for some time. After the Black September of 1970, in which Palestinian forces were liquidated by the Jordanian Army, he went to France. In an interview with Robyn Creswell for *The Paris Review*, Khoury tells us that during his study of Social History at the École Pratique des Hautes Études in Paris where he wrote a thesis on the Mount Lebanon Civil War of 1840-1860 (between the Maronite Christians and the Druze [The Druze are an ethno-religious group in Lebanon who self identify as Unitarians]), he found that there were no written accounts of the war. There were only whispers about a Christian murdering a Druze or a Druze killing a Christian. Khoury believed that such accounts were important to understand one's present and to make sense of it. He tells us, "to have a present, you have to know which things to forget and which things to remember. Our lack of written history made me feel that I didn't even know the country I grew up in. I didn't know my place in it" (Interview).

When Khoury began writing his novels during the civil war in Lebanon that broke out in 1975 and in which he fought as a militant on the Palestinian side, he chose to write about the war, about the present, as the narrator of *Kingdom of Strangers* declares: "I learned that stories are told because they are known, and that, when they tell their stories to each other, people transform the past into the present. Stories exist solely for the purpose of making the past present" (Khoury 5). Khoury, thus, started writing about the war in which he was fighting on the side of Fatah, Lebanese National Movement (LNM) and other allies. LNM supported Palestine Liberation Organization (PLO), to which Fatah was affiliated, for its right to pursue the liberation struggle from Lebanon (Traboulsi 200). They fought against the Lebanese Front including Phalange party, a political party of Maronite Christians in Lebanon, and their allies who were against the PLO operating from Lebanon.

The civil war is known to have been triggered by the Ayn al-Rummaneh bus incident of 13 April 1975. On this day, a congregation of Phalange supporters in front of a church in Ayn al-Rummaneh, a locality in East Beirut, was shot at by unidentified gunmen, injuring a number of people. The Phalangist militiamen reacted, on the same day, by firing at a bus heading for the Tall al-Zatar Palestinian refugee camp in East Beirut that killed twenty-one Palestinians. Fighting broke out between the Phalangists and the Palestinian resistance groups as well as their Lebanese allies in South-East Beirut (Traboulsi 183). Thus started the civil war in Beirut in 1975 and continued for fifteen years punctuated by short ceasefire periods and this is the context in which most of Khoury's novels are set.

Elias Khoury published his first novel *An Ilaqat al-Dairah* in Arabic in 1975. Except this novel, all of his novels have been translated into English. A few of them have also been translated into French and German. Khoury published his second novel *Little Mountain* in 1977 (translated into English in 1981) when he was also fighting with *fedayeen* (plural of *feda'i*) in the Lebanese Civil War. In this novel, Khoury describes the war as it was happening. The narrators in the novel are not clearly distinguished from one another but all of them are *fedayeen* fighting in the war except for one chapter that depicts the war from a Lebanese citizen's point of view. Khoury speaks about writing this novel in these words: "And honestly, after I finished writing it, I was afraid because I didn't know what I'd done. I didn't know what to call it. . . . All I knew at the time was that we had to do the opposite of what Arab writers did in the nineteenth century. Instead of historical novels, we needed to write things as they happened, to tell the story of the present." (Interview)

Little Mountain therefore describes the conflict in a highly fragmented manner, non-coherent and non-linear way. The form of the novel embodies the form of the war. It describes disjointed moments of fighting in a church near Bab Idriss Square in downtown Beirut, a scene of fighting on a snow-covered mountain, fragments of dialogues of *fedayeen* with one another and Father Marcel in the church, a citizen's view of his life in war, allusions to the French colonization of Lebanon, reminiscences of Lebanese students' protests and so on. It depicts the passion and ideals of young men fighting for social justice and freedom of poor from oppression.

Khoury is writing from within a war which is still unfolding. There is a critical consciousness in the novel in the form of a *feda'i* who is not named but who is fighting but at the same time criticizing and pointing to the contradictions and complications as they emerge in the war. This self-criticism is one of the prominent characteristics of Khoury's work. The capacity for self-criticism is a composite element of a revolutionary consciousness for him. That is why Khoury's protagonists do not shy away from reflecting on their actions, admitting their disappointments and weaknesses. Thus, a critical consciousness starts emerging in *Little Mountain* and continues through other novels. As this critical consciousness starts waning in the *fedayeen*, the war becomes more and more senseless and absurd. Khoury writes, "Literature, in our situation must put together two elements: seeing and inventing; it must tell the truth and lie; it must combine the real and the fantastic at the same level and at the same moment" (qtd. Gana 525). This simultaneous "seeing and inventing" is embodied in the critical consciousness of the *feda'i* who relates the war as it unfolds.

The *fedayeen* are mostly university students who protested on the streets of Lebanon in the late 1960s and early 1970s demanding social reforms and supporting the Palestinian Liberation Organization's right to operate from Lebanon. The narrator of *Little Mountain* recounts, "It was just after April 23, 1969. The pools of blood then coating the streets of Beirut signalled the onset of the torrent of blood that was later to convulse the city" (127). The incident refers to the cabinet crisis in Lebanon that was followed by increasing tension between the Lebanese state and the PLO. Fawwaz Traboulsi, the Lebanese historian and political scientist, in his book *A History of Modern Lebanon*, reports that on 23 April 1969, a massive demonstration of students in support of the PLO was conducted on which security forces opened fire. Many students were killed and many wounded (254). The *feda'i* in the novel reflects on these protests of which he and his friends have been a part, and observes: "I couldn't start with events. Events are ambiguous; they are distorted and not susceptible to beginnings. We started off as a triangle" (124).

The triangle refers to the three faces of this revolution. One face is represented by the students who are guided by the ideals of freedom, equality and liberation from all kinds of oppression of which the Lebanese state is a symbol. They are passionate and brave. The narrator claims that "living in the constant discovery of everything, in the nothingness of everything . . . is revolution. It is always beginning in spite of politics or inside of politics" (123-24). These students are beaten and trampled upon by coercive forces of the state but they show no reverence for the establishment. However, they did not know at that time that it was the beginning of the war as the *feda'i* narrator of *Little Mountain* reflects retrospectively: "What we didn't realize then was that the war had begun. Then it spread to Ghandour, to the killings. Then it was ablaze and it stayed that way" (128). Ghandour here refers to the demonstrations of workers in confectionaries who joined students' protest. During their peaceful protest in 1972, police fired on them and many were killed.

Another face of this revolution is represented by the character Dr. Hanna, a professor of Psychology who would talk about his poor childhood when he worked in a cloth store in Souq Sursock, a prominent commercial area of Beirut. He would not teach psychology but lecture students about Marxism and Dialectics and his solidarity with the poor and downtrodden. The students admired him and listened to him for three years. They were so inspired by his lectures that the contempt and intolerance for oppression took root in their hearts and minds but when the time to resist came, the professor betrayed them. The professor had projected himself as a radical but when the police came to arrest radicals, he ran away and the narrator mockingly says that he became dedicated to psychology from then on. Dr. Hanna represents the people or academia who only pay lip service to the revolutions of change who Khoury is critical of. For him, a revolution begins with an idea to change but it needs everyone's effort to work for that change.

The third side of the triangle is represented by students like Yaaqub who are brave but lack commitment. He is a philosophy student who would lead the demonstrations and face police brutalities. But he is not committed to revolutionary ideals. Even though, he becomes a *feda'i*, he gives it up to study in Europe. For Khoury, ideology and commitment are both important for revolutions to succeed. What started as a triangle exploded into circles partly because of the lack of commitment on the part of the people like Dr. Hanna and Yaaqub.

Elias Khoury sets out to show how one of the faces of the triangle, that is, the students including Khoury, who remained committed to the revolutionary ideals were caught up in the civil war. As their peaceful demonstrations were brutally suppressed, they went to take up arms and became *fedayeen*. The young men named Talal, Salem, Jaber, Ahmed, Atef and so on fighting in the civil war see themselves as revolutionaries who believed in the liberation of the oppressed. They are full of passion and lively energy carrying their guns like children playing with their toys because they believe they will be victorious in changing the world and that they are fighting a war to end all wars. For them, "victory means that the poor become the masters and the former remain masters but without serfs. The organ will play an eastern mode and our fingerprints will be the flag" (38). They want to liberate Lebanon from sectarian forces, and then defeat Israel and America which are projected as fascists. The *fedayeen* are revolutionaries in the making. Amidst fierce battles on the streets, these young men discuss war, ask questions, answer them or left them unanswered depending on the exigencies of the battle. This is a way to keep thought alive and not to give in to the violence for the sake of violence. They are aware that war destroys things but they believe it will end all wars and oppression. The lyricism of the prose in *Little Mountain* complements and reflects the fervour and passionate energy of these young men.

When these *fedayeen* were earlier sent to Amman to fight, they were pleased with themselves and full of pride. That was supposed to be their first taste of the fight. So strong were their ideals and convictions that some of them were furious when they were given a prison hall to sleep in for the night because of space constraint as they were hundreds in number. Salem bursts out, "we're in the prison. We came to fight and find ourselves in the prison. On principle, I don't agree. We can't sleep in the prison even if it's empty. . . . A *feda'i* can't sleep in prison" (74). Another *feda'i* named Talal finds it 'magnificent' to start the revolution from the prison. They were romantics who believed in the romantic idea of a hero who delivers the world from evil. Talal finds it even more suitable and fitting to start from the prison when he tells his comrade: "revolution is beginning from the prison. I don't think it was planned but it's happening as if it were. It's as if it were saying that it's a prison which will destroy all prisons" (74). This revolution is the hope of Palestinians too. This is presented in the novel through a Palestinian *feda'i* Saqr Quraish who had witnessed the Arab-Israeli war of 1967 in which Arabs were miserably defeated and which disclosed the resolve of the Arab states to fight oppression and occupation. He remembers the farce of that war in which Arabs were ill-prepared with their outdated weapons (60). He feels that the war that they are fighting in, that is the Lebanese Civil War, is better than that of 1967. Khoury himself points to this when he recalls his days with the *fedayeen* and says, "we believed we were the vanguard of a wider Arab revolution. None of us were so stupid as to think we could liberate Palestine while the whole Arab world was ruled by dictators" (Interview).

However, as the *fedayeen* continue to fight and the war prolongs, a sort of weariness sets in. They all knew that they were going to die but they had not seen death before. Now they see their comrades dying and they see nothing heroic about it. It is not even a natural death. "I am talking because I'm sad" (77) is how one of the *fedayeen* reacts to death. They keep on talking to each other endlessly because they are sad yet have to put up a heroic face to fight on. They have come to realize that the war is not going to end. One of the *fedayeen* reflects on their history and says:

> We're dying like flies. Ever since the Mongols, may be just before or after them, we've been dying like flies. Dying without thinking. Dying of disease, of bilharzia, of the plague, in childbirth or the absence of childbirth. We are dying like flies. Without any consciousness, without dignity, without anything. (77)

They begin to realize that their victory is precarious. It is "a tattered robe . . . we can touch victory but we cannot hold onto it" (68). The betrayal of their ideals is suggested even before they have joined the civil war. When they were sent to Amman to fight, they came to know, after staying in the prison hall for three days, that no battle was going to take place because the "objective conditions weren't ripe" (48); they were sent back to Beirut. This is a reference to the Jordanian Army's massacre of the Palestinians in 1970. This suggests that their optimism and idealism were not enough to make a revolution. There were forces beyond them, "the objective conditions" that were not in their control.

The *feda'i* who has survived the civil war reflects later that the revolution failed or was left incomplete. When the triangle exploded into circles, the revolution began to lose the form and purpose. It transformed into an endless and purposeless violence that is emphasized in Khoury's novels through repetitive style of his prose. The *feda'i* has affinity with the author himself who criticizes the revolution from within and depicts its contradictions without smoothing them out. Khoury describes his experience with the *fedayeen* as a "kind of training for life, and for death" that "required the utmost ethical commitment and the ability to see things critically, even at times ironically," which he believes is "common to most people who are caught up in trying to make a revolution" (Interview). It becomes possible for the *feda'i* to assess their achievements when the war stops for some time and he looks at it retrospectively and feels that they have not been able to destroy the structures of oppression completely as he tells us: "When they announced the war was over and published pictures of the terrible devastation that had been visited upon Beirut, we discovered that we hadn't destroyed it. We had made a few breaches in its ramparts but she wasn't destroyed. New wars are probably needed to do that." (135)

The destruction of Beirut here is the destruction of the traditional system of exploitation of poor by those in power. The *feda'i* understands that the revolution would have succeeded if they had destroyed everything to create anew. It is retrospectively that he is able to see what more is required but there is no longer that strong conviction which characterized the university protests. That is why when he thinks that "next time, we shouldn't content ourselves with stealing the rope, we should break it; next time, we shouldn't content ourselves with overrunning the squares and the buildings, we should destroy them" (140), there is a conditional clause on which this endeavour depends, that is whether there will be a "next time."

The figure of *feda'i* in *Little Mountain* is not a mindless militant armed with guns. He is well-educated and steeped in history. While he is able to criticize and reflect on the war in which he participates, he is also familiar with the European colonization that is known to have transformed the Arab world. He knows that the civil war has its roots partly in the European colonization of the Arab world. Khoury suggests that Lebanese Christians shared in the larger Arab identity. They did not see themselves as part of the European Christianity. For example, when Egypt defeated Israel, United Kingdom and France and gained control over Suez Canal in 1956, both Christians and Muslims in the Arab world rejoiced and celebrated the victory. Then suddenly in 1958, the narrator remembers, differences between Christians and Muslims emerged. He recounts, "barricades in the neighbourhood. Sombre faces. The Muslims want to kill us. My mother didn't believe it. She always said that's crazy. They're very much like us" (11). The year 1958 is the year when United Arab Republic was declared, and Britain and America realized that "oil was in jeopardy" (Traboulsi 136), they started interfering in the politics of the Middle East. One way to intervene was inciting sectarianism.

Sectarian violence helps to cover up Euro-American and Zionist interests in the Arab world. A Lebanese critic and scholar, Noori Gana, argues that the portrayal of the Lebanese Civil War (1975-1990) as "religious" and "sectarian" "not only exonerates Western imperialism and its unexorcised legacies but also obscures the incubational historical moments of which the war is a product—namely, the *nakba*, or catastrophe of 1948 and the *naksa*, or setback of 1967, both of which resulted in the Zionist expropriation and occupation of Arab land" (506). Khoury shows that the civil war in Lebanon that was thought to be caused specifically by the presence of the Palestinian fighters in Lebanon, is not as simple as it appears. The war continued for ten years even when the Palestinian *fedayeen* were ousted from Lebanon.

The *fedayeen* show the awareness of this fact in their discussion of the Eastern Question. One of the *fedayeen* called Nazeeh in *Little Mountain* tells others that "the Eastern Question must be settled once and for all. For three hundred years now the West has been driving the knife into our side in the name of the Eastern Question and the rights of minorities. We should be done with the question for good" (71). The Eastern Question, in diplomatic history, refers to the concern of European powers about their strategic and political interests in the Arab world when the Ottoman empire began disintegrating in the nineteenth century. At that time, the weakening of the Ottoman empire was seen as beneficial for Imperial Russia while it was considered inimical to the interest of others like the Great Britain.

Though the civil war continues to be a substance or medium in which the subsequent novels of Khoury are interwoven, the critical consciousness of the *feda'i* becomes less pervasive as we progress from one novel to the other chronologically. By this I mean, the war is now looked at largely from the eyes of those for whom the *feda'i* believed they were fighting, that is the marginalized and downtrodden. In fact, the *feda'i* figure in *Little Mountain* who was full of idealism and optimism himself becomes a marginalized figure in subsequent novels. This marginalized figure appears as Fahd Badreddin in Khoury's third novel *White Masks* that was published in 1981. The immediate context of the novel is the first six years of the Lebanese Civil War that lasted from 1975 to 1990 with small intermittent periods of ceasefire. The *feda'i* who looks at the civil war retrospectively in *Little Mountain* is from Beirut, that is, he is a Lebanese citizen. But Fahd is a twenty-six-year-old Palestinian *feda'i* who has fought with Joint Forces (Fatah and its allies in Lebanon) against the Phalangists, the Right-wing Christian Militia of Lebanon. Fahd is a student of Arabic literature at the Lebanese University but he has suspended his studies due to the injury to his eyes during fighting. His right eye is artificial because it was damaged in a battle on a mountain top that is also referred to in *Little Mountain*. Owing to his injury, he is not deemed fit to fight, therefore, he spends his time at the party office in Wata Mussaytbeh in West Beirut. Since he has no relatives or acquaintances in Beirut, he also sleeps at the party premises. The truth is that he is not considered fit for fighting because he has been critical of the Joint Forces the organization is a part of. By examining the civil war critically Khoury, in this novel, criticizes the organization of which he had been a part.

Fahd belongs to that generation of the *fedayeen* who had ethical commitments, who believed they would "hold the sky between their fingers" (182), that they would free the world from all kinds of misery and oppression. But as the war continued, the hope to create a free world started disappearing. Fahd relates an incident about his battalion capturing a seventeen-year-old boy fighting on the Phalangist side during a battle. Fahd interrogates him and finds that he did not know why he had been fighting. He was just a poor kid who had no idea of what he was fighting for with the Phalangists. But the commander of his unit Comrade Omar kills him in cold blood. He kills him in revenge because the Phalangists kill *fedayeen* when they capture them. Fahd considers it cruel, an absolutely unnecessary action. What enrages him further is that they did not bury him but left his body to decay. When he tells the commander that the dead should be buried, the commander thinks he is unreasonable. He tells him, "You're a war casualty, and your injury has undoubtedly affected your morale. Go back to Beirut and rest up" (208) and Fahd is sent back. Burying the dead is one of the greatest principles of humanity. Fahd believes that the opponents in the war should stop fighting and give each other time to bury their dead but even this ethical principle is not respected in the absurdity of this war.

The *feda'i* in *Kingdom of Strangers* has realized that the storyteller dies but the story continues. He is conscious of the responsibility of being a witness to what happened. Therefore, he becomes a writer who is writing stories, writing his memories and reflecting on the writing of stories, with a refrain "What am I writing about?" (9) He is trying to find out how to tell the stories of other *fedayeen*, the stories of the civil war, the stories of the different massacres of Palestinians and their sufferings in the refugee camps of the Lebanon.

The *feda'i* like Khoury himself has become a writer struggling to tell the story partly to find some meaning in chaos as he says, "We find stories tossed in the streets of our memory and the alleys of our imagination. How can we bring them together, to impose order on a land in which all order has been smashed to pieces?" (84) It is above all the story of the struggle in telling the story. Even though the narrator is aware of some flaw in the story, he might not have told the story the way it should have been told but he has stood witness to what he saw, to the stories that should have remained untold. Thus, he declares:

> I am the one who saw,
> I bear witness, and I say, and I shout
> I am the one standing on the shore of the Dead Sea,
> Where the mirrors and the copper faces are, where the earth is separated from the earth. (103)

Thus, the *feda'i* is finally transformed into a witness who survived to do the telling as Fatima Fakhro, the widowed caretaker in *White Masks* puts it: "if someone survived to tell the tale there'd never be another war" (259).

Works Cited

Gana, Nouri. "Formless Form: Elias Khoury's *City Gates* and the Poetics of Trauma," *Comparative Literature Studies*, vol. 47, no. 4, 2010, pp. 504-32.

Khoury, Elias. "Elias Khoury, The Art of Fiction No. 233," Interview by Robyn Creswell. theparisreview.org.

_____. *Little Mountain,* trans. Maia Tabet. New York: Picador, 2007.

_____. *The Kingdom of Strangers*, trans. Paula Haydar. Fayetteville: U of Arkansas P, 1996.

_____. "The Necessity to Forget and Remember," Interview by Sonja Mejcher. *Banipal 12*. http://www.banipal.co.uk/selections/48/151/elias-khoury

Traboulsi, Fawwaz. *A History of Modern Lebanon*. London: Pluto Press, 2007.

Machismo and Women's Subversion: A Study of Gabriel Garcia Marquez's *Chronicle of a Death Foretold* and Shauna Singh Baldwin's *What the Body Remembers*

TANVIR SACHDEV
S.C.D. Govt. College, Ludhiana

Hispanic as well as Indian cultures have largely been male dominated and place great value on pride, honour and an exaggerated sense of masculinity. Machismo emphasizes the dominance of males in both social and familial roles in both cultural contexts. Pantiz defines machismo as "an ethos comprised of behaviours prized and expected of men in Latin American countries" (qtd. Miguel et al 20). According to Miguel machismo comprises both positive and negative connotations. The positive aspects deal with "caballerismo" or a "code of masculine chivalry" that focuses on "social responsibility" to the family (20). Its negative aspects comprise of the domination of women, sexism, and aggressive hyper masculine behaviour. The paper compares the codes of machismo, the cultural ethos and the strategies of women's subversion in Gabriel Garcia Marquez's *Chronicle of a Death Foretold* and Shauna Singh Baldwin's *What the Body Remembers.* The circumscribed world of women is analyzed, where they are seen as the epitome of the honour of their families. Marquez's world of honour and orthodox Catholic ideals of chastity and purity that lead to violence and murder, are juxtaposed with Baldwin's colonial world that teaches shame to its daughters, where women are killed for honour and valued only for their ability to bear children. In *What the Body Remembers* too, women become the site on which issues like men's honour, children and claims of the community become deciding factors. In both the texts, the private world of women's honour is negotiated in the public domain by men. The intersecting oppressions of class and gender are also examined. Yet in the liminal spaces, women negotiate their subversion, either through transgression or incitement. The various dynamics at work and the resistance that women adopt to build an independent space for themselves under such an oppressive system are explored.

The male characters in the text conform both to positive and negative aspects of machismo expected of them. In its "caballerismo" or positive aspect, machismo as social construct demands the men to be providers and protectors with familial and social responsibility. Furthermore masculinities are reinforced by cultural codes of society that link them to weaponry, community, and sexuality. In both the texts men conform to this cultural code. In *Chronicle* Santiago Nasar opts out of college to look after his family ranch after his father's death, the Vicario twins also display family responsibility after the blindness of their father. Similarly, in *What the Body Remembers* the male characters take up their family responsibility seriously—Bachan Singh, Roop's father, provides not only for his own family but extended family as well, his widowed son-less mother-in-law, his unmarried cousin, Revati Bhua; Sardarji is proud of his generosity to his two wives, showering them with gold necklaces, three-tiered earrings with diamonds and Burmese rubies. Santiago in *Chronicle* has a proclivity for weapons. "From his father he learned at an early age the manipulation of firearms, his love of horses, and the mastery of high flying birds of prey, but from him he also learned the good arts of valour and prudence" (6). He is an excellent shot and can with his magnum .357 cut a horse in two through the middle and always carries arms, and even sleeps with a loaded pistol under his pillow. His association with varied firearms—a Malincher Schonaure 30.06 rifle, a Holland magnum 300 rifle, a Hornet .22 with telescopic sight, a Winchester repeater further reinforce this machismo. Sikh machismo also reflects men's fondness for weapons. Roop's brother Jeevan habitually cleans his father's 303. Sardarji's pistol, that he carries during partition reinforce the construct of men as protectors not only of women but also of community.

Sikh Machismo during partition comprises not only of an exaggerated sense of personal masculinity but extends to include the pride and honour of the entire Sikh community as well as the nation. Thus Sardarji fulfils his obligation not only to his *quom*/ community despite its eviction from what becomes Pakistan with money that reinforces the "war chests of the Akalis" with kirpans, spears and unlicensed guns, and ammunition for Sikh soldiers but also to the nascent nation—carrying secretly, at great peril to himself files and papers of projects of irrigation canals (453): "How could he continue building in the face of anger, violence and death—and why should he worry . . . because . . . building and maintaining are what administrators do . . . inventing the future slowly, building on the past" (455).

This sense of male pride, assumes another dimension with Sardarji who pictures "God not as the ten Gurus saw it, but in his own image; a rational maleness whose high position demands that he dedicate himself to keeping the mainspring of the universe wound up and ticking" (265).

Male sexuality, particularly promiscuity, is celebrated as an important aspect of machismo in both Hispanic and Indian cultures. Santiago along with several men who visit the brothel of Maria Alexandria Cervantes is celebrated for gaining sexual experience and knowledge. "I was recovering . . . in the apostolic lap of Maria Alejandrina" (3). Santiago's "fierce" sexual desire, illustrated by his close scrutiny of his cook Victoria Guzman and her daughter Divina Flor as they work in the kitchen, ('without taking his eyes off the two women' [7]) and his advances towards them augment sexist aspects of machismo. Like his father Ibrahim Nasar who had seduced Victoria Guzman for several years in the stables and brought her to the ranch to work as a house servant when his liaison with her is over, Santiago is a womanizer. His amorous advances towards her daughter, Divina Flor are aimed to "tame" the girl "overwhelmed by the drive of her glands" (8). In fact the metaphors of hunting and falconry underscore sexist codes that govern the society in both the texts. Santiago is compared to a "chicken hawk" that "nipped the bud of any wayward virgin" he could find (90-91).

Similarly Sardarji in *What the Body Remembers* indulges in polygamy to have a male heir for his vast estate. When his first wife Satya remains childless after several years of marriage he marries sixteen-year-old Roop, twenty-six years his junior. His discreet exploits with the working class pretty Kitty during his Oxford years are part of the sexual permissiveness that machismo provides. The male sexual prowess is underlined once again with the twirl of his moustache when he looks at his beautiful young wife or when he "prowls" Roop's chambers like a hunter when he finds her missing. Hunting and falconry imagery along with the metaphor of "falcon eyes" is used to bring out machismo.

In Marquez's world, colonization saw the infiltration of orthodox Catholic ideals of chastity and purity into the relatively permissive and equal local tradition. The code of machismo and honour cannot be segregated from intersecting oppressions of class and race. Both Marquez and Baldwin present complex forces at work, and the strategies of subversion and resistance that women adopt to negotiate an autonomous space for themselves under such an oppressive system. Both the authors thus critique a system that allows no space for assertion of women's choices. The female subjects in both the texts have suitors of high social standing. Angela's suitor Bayardo is the son of a legendry General of the Civil Wars and Roop's suitor Sardarji is a member of the elite civil service as well as a rich landowning jagirdar. Bayardo San Roman's courtship of Angela Vicario, via the rituals of Latin American marriage, highlights the paradigms of class. In fact class and wealth become a powerful hegemonic force that robs women of their choice and agency. This courtship ritual of giving expensive gifts—a mother-of-pearl inlay music box or buying all the raffle tickets, or procuring widower Xius' house for ten thousand pesos because she likes it—serve but not validate Bayardo's love for Angela; it demonstrates the man's affluence and power. Angela's protestation about lack of love or her objection, that he was "too much of a man" for her is brushed aside by the decisive argument that "a family dignified by modest means had no right to disdain that prize of destiny" (34). Her dislike of his public avowal of affection by disarming her family with his charm and position is rejected by a cryptic "Love can be learned" (34). At the same time, it cannot be dismissed that class becomes a paradigm in the death of Santiago. A man of fortune is othered by his wealth and ethnicity, as he is an Arab. In fact the butcher, Faustino Santos, questions as to why Santiago Nasar had to be killed for there were so many other *rich people* who deserved dying first.

In *What the Body Remembers*, although no courtship rituals permeate the Indian arranged marriage scene, Sardarji is positioned as the Jagirdar, a man of power with his turban high and proud, who has Roop's father pinned down under thirty seven percent interest by his brother-in-law—a fact that makes him a suitor who cannot be refused. Neither Roop nor Angela are given a choice in the marriage though Roop is eager to settle down for pretty clothes with a man 27 years her senior, "a man who laughs like that, . . . with no snickering hesitation in case . . . anyone be offended, a man in control, a man who can make a woman's life easy" (152). Both Marquez and Baldwin critique a system where the question of women's choice is annulled under the twin oppressions of both class and gender.

In *Hidden Histories of Gender and the State in Latin America*, Elizabeth Dore and Maxine Molyneux have emphasized older women's role within the extended family as "reinforcing patriarchy" (242). Woman such as Purisima, Angela's mother internalized these value systems, became "active agents for perpetuating patriarchal norms" thereby raising her daughters to get married. Angela in *Chronicle* grows up "under the rigour of a mother of iron" (37). Even after she is engaged to Bayardo for two months, she is not allowed alone with her fiancé but her mother and blind father accompany her "to watch over her honour." "Any man will be happy with them because they've been raised to suffer" (31). Reared to get married they embroider, sew, weave bone lace, wash and iron and tend to the sick, Angela has a helpless air and a poverty of spirit. Thus, women internalize these codes of chastity, honour and surveillance, exposing the mechanics of patriarchal power at the most intimate levels of women's experience.

The question of 'honour' associated with women's sexuality and the surveillance and regulation that it entails are closely linked to the concept of machismo. According to Ritu Menon and Kamla Bhasin, women are objects in "*male constructions of their own honour*. Women's sexuality symbolizes 'manhood'; its desecration is a matter of such shame that it has to be avenged" (43, my italics). Raised under strict surveillance, women are seen as flag-bearers of the honour of their families in an ethos where "there is no public misfortune more shameful than for a woman to be jilted in her bridal gown" (41). Angela's sexual misconduct of having pre-marital sex is punished by returning her to her family on the wedding night. It is inexorably linked to machismo for when she names Santiago as the perpetrator, the Vicario twins are forced to avenge her honour by performing the “horrible duty” of killing him (57). Thus avenging Angela’s honour becomes a criterion for the constructions of male machismo where the Vicario brothers are obliged to “prove their status as men” (84). The protection and vengeance of a woman’s honour in fact endorses male aggression and machismo. Marquez exposes how the cultural codes of women’s chastity and honour are part of a larger system for exploitation that sanctions senseless violence of which both men and women become victims. Marquez uses the close knit community to emphasise the power of public-held codes. Such is the pervasive power of the honour and machismo, that the murder is executed despite the fact that “no one really believes that it really had been Sanitago Nasar” (90). Yet no one tries to prevent it. Even the account of Angela’s naming him is shrouded in mystery. “She found it at first sight among the many, many easily confused names from this world and the other” (47). It is because the belief system of honour and machismo is shared by the entire community that town people accept Santiago’s murder as inevitable. It is accepted without question that Angela’s honour has been taken and must be avenged by killing Santiago. "But most of those who could have done something to prevent the crime and didn’t do it, consoled themselves with the pretext that affairs of honour are sacred monopolies, giving access only to those who are part of the drama" (98). Further the Vicario twins describe their deed to the judge as “homicide in legitimate defence of honour . . . that they would have done . . . a thousand times over for the same reason” (48). The fact that the belief system is shared by the entire town is further reinforced by the fact that the judicial system reduces the sentence to three years. Women also share this code of honour and machismo. Prudencia, Pablo’s fiancé, declares that she would have never even considered marrying the man “if he hadn’t done what a man should do" (63). Almost all the characters in the story including authority figures of the patriarchal state institutions like the military, civil administration, the church reveal their complicity in the impending murder as they know about it yet none of them warn Santiago. "The unquestioning acceptance of the murder and the collective unwillingness to avert its course raises larger questions on the imperviousness born out of the everyday experience of violence perpetrated by state apparatuses in Latin America on its people under both its colonial and postcolonial histories" ("Women").

However in this dominant discourse of machismo and honour runs, as Foucault points out, a counter-discourse of resistance. Foucault in the *History of Sexuality* argues: "where there is power there is resistance. . . . There is a plurality of resistances . . . that are possible, necessary, improbable" (95-96). In fact seemingly powerless subjects also exercise power through day-to-day resistances. Even powerless women like Victoria Guzman and her daughter Victoria Flor, who are victims of Santiago and his father's sexism, employ subversive strategies by choosing to remain silent rather cautious Santiago, for in "the depths of her heart she wanted to kill him" (11). Similar gestures of subversion against established hegemonies of the church, the state, and society that sanctions forms of violence can be seen in women's small everyday resistance. Santiago's mother, Placido Linero's refusal to wait for the bishop: "He won't even get off the boat. He will give an obligatory blessing, as always and go back the way he came. He hates this town," in a way challenges the authority both of the church as well as the colonial state that supports it. The narrator's mother too subverts autocratic conservative regime by refusing to meet General Patronio San Roman, the proclaimed 'hero' of the civil wars, for he was "the man who gave the orders for Gerineldo Marquez to be shot in the back" (33). Apart from Santiago's mother, Clotilde Armenta is the solitary woman who makes several attempts to prevent his murder. She appeals to the Vicario twins to leave him "if only out of respect for His Grace the Bishop," urges Bedoya to warn Santiago, informs the bishop and the Mayor (14). In fact her persistent endeavour is in fact a staunch subversion of senseless code of honour and machismo as well as the violence it sanctions. Her lamentation about the solitariness of women on her failure to prevent a murder, for which the entire community is collectively responsible, highlights the lack of agency of women that makes resistance to archaic codes of violence and honour problematic. Nonetheless through these gestures women negotiate a small space for resistance that allows their assertion of choice and opinion.

However it is Angela who charts a bold and novel trajectory of subversion by her refusal to conform to the stereotypical roles set by the codes of honour and machismo. Despite her apparent docility and lack of power visible in her coercion to get married to Bayardo, her non-virgin status becomes a sign of everyday resistances that Foucault talks about. Angela's choice not to be a virgin till she gets married is a conscious mode of resistance to the hegemonic honour and machismo code by which the Hispanic culture is governed. Moreover her refusal to fake her virginity—by resorting to old wives tricks of feigning embarrassment, taking a douche of alum water "for it was dirty and shouldn't be done to anybody, is a subversion of the puritan code that enforces celibacy and purity of women" (92). Furthermore in her naming and not naming the real perpetrator is a conscious choice of protecting the one she really loved. "She would recount her misfortune in full details to anyone who wanted to hear it, except for one item which would never be cleared up—who was the real cause of her damage and why, because no one believed that it had been really Santiago Nasser" (90). Moreover her refusal to reveal her non-virgin status is read by the narrator's mother as an "act of courage" in skillfully playing "her marked cards until the final consequence" that reduces Bayardo's machismo, class and power to a pitiable status, "the poor man who had the bad luck to marry" her (92). By her refusal to conform to the conduct of a fallen woman after she is brought home in disgrace on the night of her wedding, Angela creates a space for subversion. She refuses to live in shame and guilt and in fact becomes a self-realized individual making her own choices: "she became lucid, overbearing, mistress of her own free will . . . . She recognized no other authority than her own nor any other service than that of her obsession" (94). Mistress of her life for the first time, she becomes an embroiderer with financial independence, buys a house with a large courtyard and good cross-ventilation. Her relentless and delirious pursuit of Bayardo with two thousand feverish letters written to him over twenty years, "of the eternal scars he had left on her body, the salt of his tongue, the fiery furrow of his African tool," is an unabashed acknowledgement of her sexuality (94). Thus through her subversion of the cultural code of the shame of discovery, she transmutes into a subject of agency, without illusions, an autonomous individual: "She was reborn" (93).

Likewise, in *What the body Remembers*, feminine honour code is centred not only on modesty and sexual shame but larger and more complex issues of community, class and nation. In Baldwin's world of partition, women become extensions of their communities and their honour is inextricably linked with the honour of the men and the nation. Thus not only is machismo/ male pride/ honour, but also the honour of the nation desecrated with the violation of women. As communal/ religious identities harden, multiple patriarchies "brand their women with their identity, inscribe their fear on their bodies, clothe them in burquas, make them badges of their honour and *izzat* and direct passions and revenge of communal frenzy on the bodies of the 'other' women" (Malik 154). Patriarchies doubly reinforced by dominant ideologies of community/ religion are inscribed on the bodies of women and ensure that Roop's friend Huma is to be clothed in "heavy woollen socks peeping out from under the hem of new black burqua" and is no longer sent to play with her (81). Women being badges of honour of men/ community are pulled out from the "private" sphere and made soft targets of communal hatred in the "public" arena of politics and the nation. Sharpening communal identities slowly give way to simmering suspicion and a frenzy of hate and revenge which is played out on the bodies of women during partition. "Women's bodies were the 'site' on which the hyper masculine revenge drama of mutual humiliation was enacted. Their bodies were the tabula on which men imprinted their bestiality" (Malik 200). Women are subjected to violence not only by men of the warring communities but also their own men to save "their" honour. Roop's father, Dipty Bachan Singh fearing that the Muslims will violate the honour of his son Jeevan's wife Kusum, beheads her with a single stroke of the *kirpan* that thc Guru had given to be raised in defence of the weak. Kusum's body is desecrated by the Muslims, used as a sign to convey a message to her husband and men of her community. Her body is brutally dismembered, each limb severed at the joint and the womb ripped out: "He received the message. Kusum's womb, the same from which his three sons came, had been delivered. Ripped out." And the message, "We will stamp your kind, your very species from existence. This is no longer merely about *izzat* or land. This is a war against your quom, for all time. Leave. We take the womb so there can be no Sikhs from it, we take the womb, leave you its shell" (511).

Jeevan Singh's response to his wife's disembodied, de-uterined corpse in lighting a pyre from petrol cans from his army jeep, becomes another sign: "That message was one that should go no further. It must be ignored that no Sikh man shows weakness or fear" (512). The bodies of women thus become the receptacle of the honour of their men, community, nation as well as the sign through which "the violent dialogue between men was conducted" (Veena Das 186).

According to Foucault, constant surveillance and examination enables a continuous and pervasive control of individual conduct. In *Discipline and Punish* he describes the way in which the central technique of disciplinary power—constant surveillance—which is initially directed toward disciplining the body, takes hold of the mind as well to induce a psychological state of 'conscious and permanent visibility' (Foucault 201). Sexual surveillance of women is effectively linked with intersecting paradigms of class: "Is it not bad enough that my granddaughter . . . is nine years old and still goes about unveiled so every sweeper knows the colour of her skin? You are not a small man. You are the *lambardar*. You must set a good example" (43). This cultural ethos dictates that Roop's mother can die rather than be sent to the hospital for fear of showing her body to strange men. Fear of outside unrelated men circumscribes Roop and her sister Madani into the interior of their father's haveli and a school with walls twelve feet high. Anxiety about Roop's chastity and purity ensures that she is chaperoned by Revati Bhua or Gujari whenever she steps outside. The cultural ethos of honour and surveillance curbs her independent, free spirit effectively so she is "raised to bend like saplings with every wind so long as it speaks with a voice of authority" (20). Her hearty appetite for food and riding her favourite horse are banned for fear that there would be no "blood on the sheets" (131). As Partha Chatterjee points out, "as with all hegemonic forms of exercise of dominance, this patriarchy combined coercive authority with the subtle force of persuasion" (248). According to Sangari and Vaid "women internalise the offered models and constitute themselves with varying degrees of conformity" —the formation of models deferred according to community/ religious identities (14). Any slight deviance from the established code of behaviour like being absorbed by civil disobedience movement and flinging her chunni into the bonfire with the protestors, can result in sanctioned forms of violence. She feels the stinging palm of her father across her cheek in a slap twice as humiliating as that of her sister, "Don't you follow outside men. You don't even know what they were saying! You could have been taken, you could have been raped, anything could have happened!" (95)

Through the discipline of surveillance Roop internalizes the codes of honour, shame and docility. She is taught through rule no. one, two and three, "the great importance of . . . chunni, her modesty, the dangers of unknown men and the importance of obedience 'for her own good'" (95). Women are taught that it is imperative for them to have dependable men --fathers/ husband/ brothers—to look after them. Nani at her deathbed advises the girls to "listen and obey your father. And your brother. There should be no difference between one and the other" (82). Effective sexual control of women assumes proportions of panic among the upper classes. Bachan Singh keeps a strict vigil over the exceptional beauty of his daughter. Roop too internalizes the codes of subjectivity expected of her:

> Roop's . . . young heart presses like a coiled steel spring against her breast. Heart that does not venture outside the haveli for fear of Bachan Singh's displeasure, heart afraid to glance at or speak to unrelated men in the village. . . . Heart that beats hard and fast as a tabla in her chest if her chunni falls but once, for a moment, to her shoulders, lest a man be smitten because Roop tempted him.
>
> By now Bachan Singh, Gujari, Revati Bhua and Kusum have done their duty well: Roop has learned shame. (128).

In Baldwin's world, dominant patriarchal definitions of a woman's role primarily as a life-bearer, allow Sardarji to be polygamous, take a second wife twenty-six years his junior, and rob them of dignity, reducing them to squabbling nerves vying for his attention. The double standards of machismo permeate the cultural ethos of colonial times where "a woman is merely cracked open for seedling like the earth before the force of the plough. If she is fertile, good for the farmer, if not bad for her" (25). Thus Satya in spite of hailing from a high-class family famous for its bravery and treating Roop as she treats her maid, Mani Mai, loses control in the private sphere because of her failure to provide an heir for Sardarji's vast wealth and property. Her own sense of guilt comes forth as "her body betrayed her every moon-month with its bleeding" and she feels, "what right had she to share his bed and bring nothing from the coupling?" (19, 21). Satya can no longer call her paternalistic patriarchy to account in recognised forms of surrogate action to intervene on her behalf: "I am not wife, for my husband has abandoned me. I'm not widow, for he still lives. I'm not mother, for the son he gave me is taken away, I'm not sister, for I have no brother. With no father, I'm but daughter of my Bebeji. And so I am no one" (360).

Schooled in these codes, Roop's fertility and fecundity becomes object of barter for the thirty seven percent interest that Roop's father owes to the moneylender, the brother-in-law of Sardarji, the jagirdar. The acceptance of the proposal becomes obligatory though couched in troupes of politeness. Roop's lack of choices is further highlighted with the appropriation of her two children by Satya, Sardarji's first wife. Her second-born, a son, is also handed over to Satya and she realizes her "obligatory altruism," that her mode of existence is reduced to a womb and she remains fixed into man-imagined construct of "Sita in her man-inscribed circle" (200).

In *What the Body Remembers* women employ strategies both direct and indirect—of individual will and rights as well as what Sangari has termed the "rhetoric of incitement" (867). Satya's soliloquy on being born a woman both times round that forms a prologue as well as the epilogue to the book is symptomatic of a subversive consciousness that survives different births. It is a rebellion against an oppressive cultural structure whose discriminative system of values condemns her to a life of humiliation as a woman: "I shriek and I curse and I rail as the midwife wraps me. . . . I am not a boy. . . . Despite a whole life of worship and expiation . . . and for all the money and temple offerings I lavished on pandits the last time around, here I am again, born a woman. . . . So angry am I. . . . If I find any of those pandits I'll tear their hearts out. Send their djinns to become insects again" (12)

Baldwin uses the dreams and magic realism to make Satya a metaphor of the unbridled, gushing, effervescent river Indus to highlight her sense of freedom and independence that is used by Vayu, with unrelenting thirst only to cast away. Satya who has "come into this world with her eyes wide open will never lower them before a man" (12). She chooses the resistance of a revolutionary direct and simple, screaming out her wronged status female rage which is manifested in her refusal to deify her husband and lower her eyes before him till "he saw himself reflected small in her grey eyes. So very small that he could not bear the image of himself" (325). Satya whose name means truth, will not bow to any imposed codes, raves and rants on Sardarji's marriage to the sixteen-year-old Roop; and taking up the rhetoric of her own rights is seen as a *churail* or the "regulatory psychobiography" of Kaikeyi (Spivak 227): "I want your love, not your duty. . . . Your fidelity, not your generosity. *I want, not for you, but for me, for myself*. Because though I failed to do what the women are for, I am still here, still your wife, still Satya. . . . *In return let me share as the Guru himself allows me, share your burdens, your obligations, your vulnerability. Let us face them, not you alone, or I alone, but you and I*" (347, my italics).

According to Sangari, in the Indian context individuality, particularly a woman's, is seen as a disruptive force since women are usually perceived as having duties; any claim to "rights" unless effectively disguised become a sign of woman's evil nature. "You have a tongue sharper than Kaikeyi. I tell you, I'm so tired of your shouting. . . . You don't want me because I tell you what you have become. I tell you what I see inside you, that's why you throw me away" (26). Satya aptly camouflages her humiliation of having the children taken away and being left at Pindi behind a mask of hauteur. Her wilful courting of death through tuberculosis cannot be read as a defeatist resignation but a final act of subversion against a world where men have not changed: "Sometimes we choose to die because *it is the only way to be both heard and seen*" (351, my italics).

Roop's trajectory of resistance, unlike Satya's cry for her own rights, charts an indirect course, where the intersecting issues of class, community and gender are played out. Roop's choice to leave Sardarji's house and go to her father is couched in delicate and indirect troupes of subversion. Her indirect agency to call upon her paternal patriarchy to account leaves a space for negotiation where her individual rights and wrongs are not evoked. The jewels that she leaves behind "inform the silence with their presence . . . a woman who leaves her ornaments leaves that unmistakable silent message that says 'I have been wronged'" (317). Sardarji comprehends the message interpreting it as "symptomatic of the moral collapse of the universe" (323). According to Sangari, "incitement exists at the interaction between the 'political' and 'domestic,' between gender relations and power relations, occupies an uneasy boundary between the respective logics of women's consent and resistance re-articulating their relationship in different ways" (872). Roop's indirect subversion plays out not only the codes of honour of men and communities but also power equations of material factors and class structures. Her fear of being poisoned by Satya is disregarded on account of men's honour and machismo: "Poison . . . is a big thing for you—you think you're so important. For Papaji *izzat* is bigger" (312). Thus her life, or dignity is of no account when weighed against men's honour.

Roop's father, Dipty Bachan Singh, is no match for Sardarji's traditional as well as modern structures of elitism. "He maybe Lambardar, he maybe Dipty of all Pari Darwaza, but in the end he is just a poor, ordinary Punjabi village man" (307). Though Roop as a "woman who has climbed beyond her father kin" has no power against structures of oppression, her brother Jeevan, as an English-educated captain in the Her Majesty's Army has moved up the social scale. It is Jeevan, with his muscles fighting fit, arms crossed, a young 'Sher' who can effectively challenge his brother-in-law. Though Sardarji realizes that Roop should fear his wrath if not his favour, in times of pre-independence turmoil, it would be useful for Sardarji to have an influential, well-disposed brother-in-law in the Army. Roop calls upon him for "the rhetoric of incitement"--her protector and saviour, for all the golden threads she has woven into rakhri for him. Jeevan as a shrewd negotiator ensures that Roop is brought back to Sardarji only when he sets up independent house for her where her children are not separated from her. Satya is now fixed as the manipulating woman or Kaikeyi who represents "control over male sexuality . . . [thus] putting male honour . . . at stake. . . . by laying him open to social castigation for being unmanly" (Sangari 873). The private world of Roop's honour and children are decided in the public domain where issues like men's honour, the children and claims of the community become deciding factors: "Best to do everything in public then at least we will all remember what was said." (328). As Sardarji comes to Pari Darwaza to settle Roop's issue, the courtyard of Bachhan Singh's *haveli* fills out with the sweet maker, the weaver, the tailor, the barber, the entire community of the Muslim dominated village with a Sikh *lambardar*. Besides larger issues of the community become deciding factors—Pari Darwaza with the dominant Muslim population has a Sikh Lambardar/ Dipty and undermining his authority as the leader of the village over a "mere woman" was something that he was not inclined to do. Thus, by setting up a structure of incitement which serves as

Roop's mode of redressal and indirect agency, she calls patriarchy as a domain of public accountability that could affect Sardarji's machismo.

Like Angela in *Chronicle*, though the trajectory of Roop's subversion traverses the indirect structure, yet it finally leads her like Angela to self-actualization worked out through magic realism that foreshadows real events. Roop's dream of walking down alone on a road with a crystal bowl filled with crimson coloured liquid, shattered into smithereens by Mrs. Barlow's sword, becomes a sign of the portioned land that wreaks havoc on the bodies of women. The red colour liquid becomes symptomatic of the "the colour of blood, . . . anguish, . . . colour of brides, of vermillion red markings of married women, blood on the sheets," inextricably linking it with honour and blood of women where they become merely sites of revenge of men's machismo and honour of the nation (421). Alone on the road to the nascent nation with her children she poses as a Muslim woman subverting the very notion of communal identities imposed upon women. It is Satya's mode of direct rebellion, humiliation and anger that she feels with empathetic identification that results in her own self-actualization. "I hold you woman within woman. Like the gurus we might be one spirit, different bodies" (422). She draws on Satya's strength and hauteur and strident voice to save her maid Jorimon from rape and death. She manages to save herself, her children and her maid. Facing the fear of Sardarji's death in the riots becomes her moment of self-actualization as she determines making her own rules without husband or custom or consequence: "I will survive even after Sardarji is gone" (424). Her proclamation of survival despite all odds becomes a sign of self-actualization and identification not only with Satya but with every woman during partition. Moved by the sight of women pulling the remnants of rags about them she drops her own clothes, making a plea to treat women as God made them, as merely human--un-inscribed by religion/ community: "Everymen, woman and child should, just once in this lifetime, see woman's body without shame. See her as no man's possession; see her, not from the corners of your eyes! . . . she wants to scream, See me, I'm human, though I'm only a woman. See me; I did what women are for. See me not as a vessel, a plaything, a fantasy, a maid servant, an ornament, but as Vaheguru made me" (498). Thus her nakedness becomes, both a political statement as well as a metaphor of the subversion of women against man-made paradigms of honour, community or nation and reaffirms their humanity and dignity despite plunder, violence and desecration.

Furthermore, both Marquez's and Baldwin's use magic realism in connection with some of his women which oppose the rationalist approaches of Western Eurocentric discourse. In *Chronicle* the narrator's and Santiago's mother's pagan beliefs and dreams; in *What the Body Remembers* Satya's references to past and future lives, spirits and *djins*, signs that they read create an aura of enigma around them. Baldwin uses dreams, the belief in transmigration, spirits, not only to critique rationalist Eurocentric discourse but also the socio-cultural structures. Satya's occupation of the liminal spaces between life and death, an immortal consciousness "floundering in the cosmos, incapable of transcending our *haumai*, our self-ness" (403) is used to critique the continuing unequal cultural ethics of society towards women that does not welcome its girl child:

> Here I wait to roll the dice again, wait for a time when just being can bring izzat in return, . . . when a woman will not be owned, when love will be enough payment for marriage, children or no children, just because my Shakti takes shape and walks the world again. (403)

> Again I am born a woman, foolish girl child. . . . The man's voice comes deep, comes low. . . . I do not need to understand words to know he is disappointed that I am not a boy. . . . I have come so far, I have borne so much pain and emptiness!
> But men have not changed. (538)

Thus both Marquez and Baldwin share the cultural ethos of machismo, honour, domination of women, shame and magic realism. Through their texts, they critique this unequal system of women's oppression and also provide a space for subversion.

Works Cited

Baldwin, Shauna Singh. *What the Body Remembers*. New Delhi: HarperCollins, 1999.

Elizabeth Dore and Maxine Molyneux, ed. *Hidden Histories of the State and Gender in Latin America.* Durham and London: Duke University Press, (2000).

Foucault, M., *Discipline and Punish: The Birth of the Prison,* trans. A. Sheridan, Harmondsworth: Peregrine, 1977.

_____, *The History of Sexuality: An Introduction,* trans. Robert Hurley. London: Penguin, 1990.

Hart, Stephen M. "Superstition, Irony, Themes," *MrQuale*. Web.

Malik, Seema. "Body as Object: A Reading of Shauna Singh Baldwin's *What the Body Remembers*," *Indian Writing in English: The Last Decade,* ed. Rajul Bhargava. Jaipur and New Delhi: Rawat, 2002.

Marquez, Gabriel Garcia. *Chronic*

le of a Death Foretold, trans. Gregory Rabassa. 1982; New Delhi: Penguin, 1996.

Miguel, G. et. al. "Toward a Fuller Conception of Machismo: Development of a Traditional Machismo and *Caballerismo* Scale," *ResearchGate*.

Sangari, Kumkum. "Consent, Agency and Rhetoric of Incitement," *Economic and Political Weekly,* 28.18 (1993) 867-82.

Sachdev, Tanvir. "Gender, Tradition and Modernity in Shauna Singh Baldwin's *What the Body Remembers*," *Guru Nanak Journal of Sociology* (2011).

Spivak, Gayatri Chakravarty. "The Political Economy of Women as seen by a Literary Critic." *Coming to Terms: Feminism, Theory, Politics*, ed. Elizabeth Weed. London: Routledge, 1989. "Regulatory psychobiographies" is a term given by Gayatri Spivak to refer to myths, legends and traditions which are deeply etched in the mind, to form the subjectivity of women. These role models and value systems are internalized to regulate the constitution of "the sexed subject."

"Women in Marquez's *Chronicle.*" *Survivingbaenglish*.

Impact of Indian Culture on Saul Bellow's *Herzog*

SONU MANISHA DANIEL
Res. Sch., School of Languages, D.A.V.V., Indore University
S.S. THAKUR
Atal Bihari Vajpayee Govt. P.G. College, Indore

In *Herzog* the protagonist is an intellectual who can analyze any situation or conception with devastating precision and irony but who is incapable of almost all simple pleasures of life. He is lost in the moral, philosophical and personal complexities of life, on which he feels compelled to give his opinion. He wants to reach reality, the easy way, through language, which is denied to him. He is advised to face internal complexity and then live with it. "You have to fight for your life. That is the chief condition on which you hold it." For this struggle the very first condition is that one must really desire to exist, to live, to say yes to face perplexities of life. In the beginning, he is not prepared to sacrifice his poor squawking, niggardly, individuality. He is conscious, that this mass civilization attracts an individual's "attainment of beauty, nobility, integrity and intensity." (204). Crushed beneath the burden of life, Herzog still advocates life and not death. He does not place suffering as highly as did Henderson: "suffering is about the only reliable buster of the spirit's sleep." Morality as whole is the area of Bellow's investigation: "where there can be no watertight compartments holding 'rights and wrongs.' This dilemma is more pronounced with American writers who are forced to deal with the chaotic modern world on its own terms, for they lack any tradition of ideas the modern epoch began."

Herzog is intellectualism personified. His total response to life is intellectual rather than instinctive. Herzog recalls with a sense of mockery and humiliation that he had tried to perform a different task of going after reality with language, trying to change reality into words. He tried to explain everything, but concludes that if unexplained life is not worth living; the explained life is unbearable too. All his efforts to explain either life or death have to be futile; he could neither resolve intellectually the complex issues of his age nor control his environment solely through its intellectual awareness. Because "life is something more than . . . mere facticity." Thus struggling hard to make coherent sense, he realizes that he is not good at it, but it is not necessary also, one can believe God and do His will without understanding Him with his concise mind. There are other subtle ways to reach God. He sends his "most loving wish" to reach out where it is incomprehensible. He can neither see nor show, neither explain nor understand but "can only pray towards it."

Herzog is clumsy, crazy, insane, utterly dejected and completely broken by female deceit and false friendship. But this specialist in suffering and spiritualism abiding by the law of the heart, retains his hopes and faith in the goodness of human heart. From a sick suffering and agitated man, he changes into a healthy happy, satisfied and relaxed person. His belief in God has strengthened his hopes for the human beings. For Herzog the soul is incomprehensible: "it lives in more elements than we will ever know" Charles Citrine in *Humboldt's Gift* comes to realize that "the soul of a civilized and rational person is said to be free but is actually very closely confined" because he is prepared to believe in nothing beyond his rational thinking mind. To Herzog the truth reveals itself in such moments that "not thinking is not necessarily fatal."

According to Indian philosophy, "the mind of a man has three aspects of the subconscious, the conscious and the super-conscious, and the 'abnormal' psychic phenomena, called by the different names of ecstasy; genius, inspiration, madness, are the working of the super conscious mind.' Human wisdom and virtues not being in demand any more life has became a total defeat: submit we must, surrender and bow down, but without hope, to the blank necessity. Thus death is the true antagonist of a modern man, it is the only God, Omnipotent unavoidable, and all-annihilating.

In *Herzog* the protagonist, who is the prince of erotic renaissance, is living in the reality of thought and words only. When his mother is dying in the kitchen, he is busy in reading *The Decline of the West* in another room. As the story advances he becomes aware of his own evil and murderous tendencies. He knows he wanted to murder Madeleine: "it's the certainty of punishment that stops me." (248)

Bellow's critics of the west extend further. The community with all its technological resources had begun to exert an overwhelming pressure upon an individual. The result is that man is reduced to a cipher. The community through its mass media brainwashes the individuals into conformity. Man had lost power to think and act for himself. He had lost his intellectual independence. He felt weak and helpless against the overwhelming forces of the community.

In *Herzog* the hero seems to be in a state of mind in which external reality cannot penetrate for any length of time. He is of the opinion that he was living in a "society that was no community and devalued the person." (248) He is unhappy over the fact that the self is here made negligible by the sheer quantities mass of the society. In a letter to President Eisen however, he suggests that society he is a distraction from more important issues. On the Malthusian pattern he formulates that "public life drives out private life." He is proud that he has become separate him from the rest of the society. The last book which Herzog looks into is by a Russian, who asserts "that private life is above everything . . . it is joy to be choked with thought" (391). But Herzog is brought to "believe that brotherhood is what makes a man human" (335). He like Leventhal comes to know that "Man liveth not by self alone but in his brother's face" (333). He is convinced now that no definition of self is complete unless it embraces other people. As the novel progresses he realizes his ungratefulness to the society in living in an imaginary human situation invested by his own genius. "How odd," he says, "But the best treated, most favoured and intelligent part of any society is often the most ungrateful" (370).

Henderson in *Henderson the Rain King* is "a reluctant type of fellow" yet bent upon seeking salvation. He knows it is "love that makes reality, reality" yet feels like not having anything "to do with husband's 'love or wife's love." So much torn between his own conflicting, paradoxical mind, that nearly for the whole length of the novel he remains confused.

Herzog ridicules the idea of facing our own death, which has been a favourite idea of the reality instructor king Dahfu. Herzog fails to make death another God in this Godless world. He rejects the German existential theory that dread saves you from distraction and gives you your freedom. He cannot agree to the thought of this generation, "nothing faithful, vulnerable, fragile can be durable or have any true power, that Death waits for these things as a cement floor waits for a draping light bulb. God neither is death, nor evil, nor is he a murderer." (182) He finds that at the bottom of all these, is the sense of a grievance. He wants nothing more to do with this. For him, it is easier not to exit altogether than accuse God. He is not going to accept victory of death over life. Death is the dark backing that a mirror needs, if we are to see anything, it compels us to utilize our life to the maximum, making it perfect day by day. Death is a common doom that comes to all and eventually takes all these destructions away between man and man, between man and things. But this should not be a reason to choose death in life, to feel the dread all along. Slowly but steadily, he moves toward a belief in the immortality of the soul which opens new possibilities in human life.

Bellow's optimism, his ultimate hopefulness, reminds one of the optimism of Indian philosophy: "The scope and freedom of Indian thought are inconsistent with an ultimate pessimism." Indian philosophy is pessimistic if by pessimism is meant a sense of dissatisfaction with what is, or exists. "Truly no optimism is worth its salt that does not go all the way with pessimism and arrive at a point beyond it."

Herzog's quest for death goes hand in hand with his introspection on contemporary society. He explains his views on every subject what concerns with the importance of human condition. Along with personal relationships, "Herzog must also do battle with mills of philosophy, law, psychology, biology and political theory" He never forgets to play the role of an intellectual thinker. Herzog the man on whom the world dependent for certain intellectual work to change history, to influence the development of civilization. Herzog liked the fumes. Sitting in dirty plush seat he took out a book and read: "For dying means that it is all over, but dying the death, means to experience the death, trying to think what this might signify. If . . . Yes . . . . No . . . . On the other hand, if existence is nausea then faith is an uncertain relief. . . . All who live are in despair. And that is the sickness unto death. It is that a man refuses to be what he is" (144).

Herzog's life would prove a different point altogether very tired of the modern form of historicism which sees in the civilization the defeat of the best hopes of Western religion and thought. The strength of a man's virtue or spiritual capacity measured by his ordinary life. Herzog says: "I believe in God-sin-death. People wish life to end. They have polluted it; courage, honour, frankness, friendship, duty, all made filthy. Sullied. There was a time when men were born, lived and died. But do you call these men? We are only creatures. Death himself must be tired of us. I can see Death coming before God to say 'what shall I do'? There is no more grandeur in Death. Release me, God from this meanness" (165-66).

It is not accidental that Herzog happened to fall in love with Mady. He is always attracted to the aggressive, masculine woman (202). "Female arrogance" excites him. Potentially sexual as well as moral masochist, he speaks metaphorically of "writhing under this sharp elegant heel." Guilt is at the root of Herzog's masochism. Here the connection is made clear: "What he was about to suffer, he deserved; he had sinned long and hard; he had earned it. And what is his sin? Essentially, it is sexual. Sex is terribly guilt producing. Twice during the novel--once in connection with Ramona, once with Mady--Herzog complains that he is a prisoner to sex. A number of times the connection between dirt and sex is made. Herzog feels sorry for Daisy who is a whore and will catch a disease. But who is a whore? There is not only sexual guilt and its association with dirt, but also conflict between illicit sexuality and his Jewish traditions. What kind of Jew is he? We have seen a number of times in Bellow's fiction the connection between sin and punishment by death—here again it is so; sex leads to death; he must wash—his hands. We understand, then, part of the reason why Moses needs to sacrifice by suffering. He is expiating his sexual sins. Braille reminds us of one character in Bellow's fiction—Augie March's blind mother. His sexual feelings for his mother are clear. It is his guilt over these feelings which leads him to masculine woman, to women who will punish him like a father. Only under such condition of punishment, only with a woman who threatens him symbolically with castration and death, can he accept his pleasure.

Ultimately it is Herzog's fear of death which is at the core of his guilt, his posturing, his ideas. In Bellow, again and again, fear of death is the root motivation; and if Herzog laughs at Tina Zokoly's theories about facing death, Bellow rejects the worship of death; but he indicates in book after book that unless you confront your death, you're worshipping it as a sacred, malign Goddess.

According to Jainism in India, "Women are looked upon as objects of temptation." They should be scorned and avoided if possible. Same is the case with Buddhism: "When Ananda asked him how a man should act in the presence of a woman, Buddha answered: "avoid looking at her . . . if it necessary to look, do not speak to her, if it be necessary to speak, then keep wide awake."

In other words, man can derive no benefit from this until he makes up his mind to observe piety and righteousness with fear of God. He has to believe in the words of his Creator about all that exists beyond his own comprehension, worship Him alone and establish His worship, believe in that has been revealed finally as well as in that which was revealed before it, and be sure of the Hereafter, that is, the day of Judgment of actions. A closer study of the *Gita* lays emphasis on piety and righteous actions and cautions against the evils of desire or the Kama. Lord Krishna proclaims it to be Arjun's duty or Swadharma. He argues with him:

> Slay thou O mighty armed, the enemy
> In the form of desire difficult to overcome

Purification of self and observance of piety are therefore recommended: "Yogis, having abandoned attachment perform action only by the body, by the mind, by the Reason, and even by the senses, for the purifications of self."

Bellow's fiction is a sensitive explanation of the post-war landscape. It shows how faith has weakened further and how technology has become even more threatening. The destructive weapons of war that man has invented are now capable of destroying the whole of mankind. It also shows the power of mass-media and how the brainwash forces the average man into conformity. Herzog thought, that his imagination of the universe was elementary. He writes a letter to Bhave: "Dear Dr. Bhave, I read of your work in *The Observer* and at the time thought I'd like to join your movement. I've always wanted very much to lead a moral, useful and active life. I never know where to begin. One can't become Utopian. It only makes it harder to discover where your duty really lies" (63). He sees the dark men going on foot through India. In his vision Herzog sees their shining eyes, and the light of spirit within them. Later Herzog saw *Pather Panchali*. "I assume you know it, since the subject is rural India. Two things affected me greatly" (64) says Herzog. It was raining also in New York as in rural India. What he had vaguely in mind was to offer his house and property in Ludeville to the Bhave movement. But what could Bhave do with it? Send Hindus to the Berkshires? It wouldn't be fair.

Herzog somehow got into a religious competition. Madeleine, Valentine Gerebach, Dr. Edvig, all talking on religion to Herzog --so he tried it out. To see how it would feel to act with humility. Herzog said, "Valentine Gersbach, brought me books (by Martin Buber) and commanded to study them." Herzog affirms the religious views of Buber: "It is wrong to turn a man (a subject) into a thing (an object). By means of spiritual dialogue, the I-Its relationship becomes an I-Thou relationship. God comes and goes in man's soul. And men come and go in each other's beds, too. You have dialogue with a man. You hold the poor fellow's hand. You give him consolation" (83, 84).

The Upanishads ask us "to lay aside our pride of intellect and self-consciousness, and approach facts with the fresh outlook of a child." Indian philosophy teaches and impels us to concentrate on the universal truth: "our enjoyment of the world is in direct proportion to our property"; "Every gain in spirit involves a loss in nature." If there was no suffering, no evil and no death, men would not be driven to ask those profound questions which illuminate their existence. The Upanishads tell us that the realization of spirit is not a smooth development or uninterrupted advance.

The Upanishads do not maintain that "intellect is a useless guide. . . . It fails to attempt to grasp the reality in its fullness." A philosophy based on intuition is not necessarily opposed to reason and understanding but "India can throw light on the dark places which intellect is not able to penetrate." It means that spiritual things require to be spiritually discerned. It maintains that the ultimate reality cannot be made into an objective representation which intellect can grasp. According to Hindu philosophy, nothing can be performed in isolation: "All perform a good action, when an evil action is performed, all perform it."

Of course, the Hindu view of universalizing individual suffering and immediate evil cannot be accepted by a rational European. It can accept both evil and good, absence and presence, chaos and unity as reality. While it has its roots in the Jewish religion, it also has close affinities with the Indian one. His closeness to Bhave or Nehru is not an accident. They show the acute awareness of the Indian moral and spiritual heritage and his attempts to reach it.

It can be concluded that Indian culture and views have great influence on Saul Bellow's writings. Bellow has effectively made use of Indian philosophy, which strongly intervenes with the ideology that there is something important which cannot be explained, that reason and rational approach lead you nowhere; consequently one withdraws himself from all mental activities and finds peace and even joy, in his merely human status. Through his characters, Saul Bellow tries to understand the meaning of the 'self' in a world of uncertainly and fluctuating magnitude. In Bellow's work, again and again fear of death is the root motivation. His works justify the spiritual dependency which prompts the sinner to think of his salvation. The Upanishads tell us that realization of spirit is not a smooth development. Of course, the Hindu view of universalizing individual suffering and immediate evil cannot be accepted by a rational European. It can accept both evil and good, absence and presence, chaos and unity as reality.

Bibliography

Saul Bellow, *Herzog*, New York: Fawcett, 1965.

_____. *Humboldt's Gift*, 427.

_____. *Henderson the Rain King*.

David Boroff. "The Author." *Saturday Review of Literature*, 19 Sept. 1964, 38, 39.

John Jacob Clayton, "Saul Bellow," *Defence of Man*, 186.

David Galloway, *The Absurd Hero in American Fiction*, 152.

Alfred Kazin, *Contemporaries*, Boston and Toronto: Little Brown, 1962, 17.

Dr. Radhakrishnan, *Indian Philosophy*, London, 1929.

T.R. Sharma. "Influence of Bhagavad Gita on Literature."

Nina A. Strees "Successor to Faulkner," Show, 4 September 1964, 38.

Age of Darkness: A Comparative Study of Dharamvir Bharati's *Andha Yug* and Erich Maria Remarque's *All Quiet on the Western Front*

POORVA GULATI
M.Phil. Scholar, G.G.S. Indraprastha University, Delhi

War has always been invested with heroic fascination and moral validation. Ages of glorious past have thought of it as an overwhelming vengeance which will redeem them, which will give them salvation, which will further safeguard their 'Dharma' and most of all which will justify their violence as the righteous Kshatriya conduct. The war is no less an age of atrocity that ends with defeat, disillusionment, fragmented psyche, disturbing discussions about the politics of revenge, moral dereliction, and the failure of a morally responsible will to intervene in acts of violation. It leaves us all with brutality of existence and invites us to hear our own complicity in evil.

Over the years, after facing rampant destruction and massive turmoil, people were struck with a realization that 'sacred', after all, does not mean to make sentimental compromises in the pursuit of Dharma, sacred does not only mean giving unnecessary sacrifices in order to be termed as a valorous warrior. The true essence of 'sacredness' lies in restoring the just balance of the world in which we live. In the face of an annihilating power, the sacred may use all the available ruthlessness that it can muster in order to survive. How a being, amidst all the chaos and turbulence, makes efforts to survive with dignity and reinforces the cause of peace where his sacredness lies.

Andha Yug, written after the carnage of partition of the Indian subcontinent, which nearly erased a form of life and civilization, which talks of the sacred, righteous war of the *Mahabharata*, and how even the sacramental war of sacrifices could not prevent the nightmares.

On the other hand, Erich Maria Remarque's *All Quiet on the Western Front* talks of the terrible brutality of First World War, which ceases to romanticize the glory of war and heroism with an unromantic vision of fear, meaninglessness and butchery. Be it the great, glorious war of the *Mahabharata* or the vulnerable First World War, these have completely altered mankind's conception of military conflict with its catastrophic levels of carnage and violence, its battles that lasted for months, and its gruesome new technological advancements (e.g., machine guns, poison gas, trenches) that made killing easier and more impersonal than ever before. Remarque's novel dramatizes these aspects and portrays the mind-numbing terror and savagery of war with a relentless focus on the physical and psychological damage that it occasions.

This paper attempts a comparative study of *Andha Yug* and *All Quiet on the Western Front* dealing with the post-war trauma and disillusionment that the two wars had on the human psyche. Remarque's work deals with hardened secular reality while *Andha Yug* gives the insight of the sacredness of this conflict, but both the works represent the slaughter of the innocent, lost to impractical dreams; they follow the trajectory from innocence to a realization of the cruelty and inhumanity of war. Remarque's *All Quiet on the Western Front* and Bharati's *Andha Yug* elucidate the dehumanizing impact of war on the psyche and the deprivable condition of veterans as 'half dead figures' who are no less than 'human animals'.

This paper studies the turmoil of a soldier when he is caught in fulfilling his duty as a warrior, but within him lays the yearning to survive amidst all the turbulence that goes on for satiating the political interests of a chosen few. It encompasses harshest critiques of Nationalism, Chauvinism and idealistic patriotism that lead to dreadful glory, that glory where there is no victory but only despair and defeat.

This paper highlights the idea that we all have descended into the Age of Darkness which has made us morally and spiritually blind. The sinister steps of our modern day politicians are no less than characters like Kantorek and Dhritarashtra, who are duplicitous in speech and action. Insatiable frenzy for power and gross materialistic actions of certain 'few' can cause rampant destruction and we are left with a split, a chasm that still torments our hearts with gnawing silences.

> There is a dark abyss in each of us, where a ferocious beast, a blind beast who is the master of all we know and do reside and has his home. (Bharati 2.55)

The 'dark abyss' or the 'blind beast' in the above lines said by Gandhari refers to the animal instinct that Remarque indicates throughout his work. This beast-like instinct is the only way for a soldier to survive battle, to turn off his mind and becoming less like a human being and more like a beast. Paul thinks of himself as a "human animal" and other soldiers who survive multiple battles operate in the same way. The experience of their battle is animalistic as soldiers trust their senses over thoughts; desires over rationality; body over mind. This animalistic instinct contributes to the larger theme that war destroys humanity of the soldier, stripping away his ability to feel and make him act in a bestial passion.

Paul and his comrades have hardly even begun with their life "in some strange melancholy way we have become a waste land," at such a tender age when their heads were forced to face and survive with the harsh reality at the front. Himmelstoss forces young boys, who want to spend the prime of their boyhood in the classroom, like other children they want to celebrate their joyous ecstasy in the charm of their youthful days. Paul and his friends were forced to join the army after listening to the stirring patriotic speeches of their teacher, Kantorek. A pompous, authoritarian schoolmaster places intense pressure on his classmates to fulfill their "patriotic duty" by enlisting in the army. This is similar to the way young Abhimanyu, son of Arjun, and Ghatotkach, son of Bheema, and five sons of Draupadi from each of the Pandavas were in a frenzy to join Dharma-Yuddha at a ripening age. Thus they succumb to the notions of death and sacrifice leading to never ending glory.

Ghatotkach in the *Mahabharata* has turned out to be a furious warrior destroying his enemy soldiers, Bheem's rival. The only duty of a neglected child was to be a warrior like his father. As a rakshasa, a being of night, his powers increased as the day waned. He fought with such an urge, that when the Kaurava warriors were at their most tired, just before trumpets announced an end to the battle day, he would fall upon them and slaughter them. The enthusiastic child warrior met his devastating end, at such an age when one should begin his trajectory, that too with Karna's whirling missile *astra*, Shakti.

Abhimanyu, another young master warrior was caught into the devastating and invincible formation of *Chakravyuha* on the thirteenth day of the war. Even the greatest Pandava warriors could not break it apart, shaped like a thousand-petalled lotus. Since there is one person in the entire Pandava army other than Arjun who knows how to penetrate vyuha and Yudhisthir, dharma manifested asked Abhimanyu to break through the vyuha. In violation of the most important code of war, the Kauravas killed his charioteer and his horses and smashed his chariot. Abhimanyu fell, at the hour of his death his eyes filled with astonishment at the perfidy of men he has respected as war heroes. Such was the glorious values of war that were taught to all the boys since the very beginning, that combating a duel, was the only primal motif for any son that was born in the royal race. Paul and his comrades like Abhimanyu and Ghatotkach, were trapped in this *Chakravyuha* of life and death at an age which for others was enthralled in youthful vigour.

There is a constant parallel between *All Quiet on the Western Front* and *Andha Yug* in the kind of dehumanizing effect war has on the life of soldiers. The men on front are subject to constant physical, mental and psychological dangers, forcing soldiers to cope with primal, instinctive fear during every waking moment. Remarque portrays the overall effect of these conditions as a crippling overload of panic and despair where in order to survive they have to disconnect themselves from their feelings, suppressing their emotions. This emotional disconnection has a hugely destructive impact on soldier's humanity. Paul becomes unable to imagine a future without the war and most importantly those who survived the war are similar to 'half dead figure', since war has such a disastrous impact on their mind that reverting to civilian life is the main difficulty in the novel. The internal destruction of these 'half dead' men in Remarque's work can be compared to 'Ashwatthama', the only saviour left from Kaurava clan thirsting for revenge on the last night of the war. The half dead figure in the two works embodies ambition instead of peace; power instead of companionship; contempt instead of hope. It is evident from the lines said by Sanjay, the prophetic narrator in *Andha Yug*, to describe Ashwatthama's physical and eternal decay, "He is hideous; his body is rotten with boils and open sours. For the sin of infanticide he is condemned to live forever, his body and mind shall fester forever. Lacerated, defiled, filthy and corrupted he shall wonder through thick and deep forests forever." (4.109)

Ashwatthama's physical decay corresponds to soldiers' mental turmoil and internal conflict after the war. Secondly,

Ashwatthama releases the 'unthinkable' weapon, the *brahmastra* whose impact once imparted cannot be taken back is similar to the effect of bombardments, barrages and hand grenades used in Remarque's war by army of both sides, creating havoc. Veterans, who have survived the brutality of First World War, are no less than Ashwatthama, who is the symbol of exhaustion of all that is ethical. His broken presence signifies that moment in the chronology of a civilization, when in complete despair, it ceases to believe that it has a future. That is why Ashwatthama becomes the raging symbol of genocide, making sure that everyone and everything on earth can be annihilated, and justify his decision to erase all traces of life as the inevitable consequences of the history he has lived. When he releases *brahmastra,* he is no less than the monster each one of us can become when afraid of losing our selfhood. The hidden doppelganger within us can purge out when we are unable to restrain our unchannelised, untamed notions of extremity. Thus Aswatthama exclaims: "I decided to turn myself into blind, ruthless and ferocious beast/ I am lost in a dark cave, the blind cave of defeat" (Bharati 67).

This is how the disastrous power of such weapons has blinded them with nothing but massive killing. The 'defeat' here refers to the defeat of humanity amidst the violence and bloodshed, defeat of peace and harmony against agitation and distress. Towards the end, when more of Paul comrades were killed, he wonders how futile war can be, even though it was clear to all the soldiers and to Paul, that they were losing the war, they were still required to fight. More recruits were dumped into battles only to die due to their inexperience. After the war there was no side of triumph, none of the side achieves anything. War succumbs to defeat, once again there is a parallel when Yudhishthira after being declared as the ruler of Hastinapur kingdom said:

> Though I won the war, a ferocious war, full of treachery, bloodshed and slaughter, I am alone and defeated, behind the throne I own stretches of long and unbroken tradition of blindness and stu-

> pidity. I tremble as I watch the encroaching darkness and hear the sinister steps of coming age and yet I must continue to live on and wear this crown. (5.140)

Paul for the first time kills a man in hand-to-hand combat. He sees the enemy to understand the true cost of taking another human being's life. The enemy he killed is not a vague figure killed from a distance but an individual with concrete identity. Paul sees the life that he destroyed and realizes that the enemy's wife and child are victims of his actions as well. This feeling of empathy is present in *Andha Yug,* when one of the Guards said:

> We are not warriors, we have shown no courage, we have not fought or showed our heroic deeds in this grim war. Our actions are meaningless, our faith, our decisions our courage, our lives are meaningless, utterly meaningless. Even after death, we shall pace the desolate corridors of Death's kingdom from right to left. (2.63)

Dhritarashtra, the blind king of the Kauravas who had the luxury of hiding behind his physical blindness for his wrong judgments can be compared to power and status hungry contemporary leaders who in order to satiate their thirst for power involve innocent folks into supporting a war that does nothing except harming them. The war is useful only to selected 'few' men who never actually went through the turmoil of combat. They are as passive and eternally blind as Dhritarashtra, lacking an inner insight. The worst part of the war is that millions of lives have been sacrificed by decision made by fewer than thirty men. Their moral blindness is evident when Dhritarashtra says to Vidura, "I was born blind, how could I have discerned the real world or recognized its social codes. I had spun an illusory world of dreams, desires and passions out of the depths of that darkness." (4.113)

War in the two works confronts the modern man with the day-to-day human dilemmas, doubts, chaos, apprehensions, and turmoil that people underwent. It encompasses an account of human conduct on everyday basis. Every man in the modern era is caught in the battlefield of 'Kurukshetra', this battlefield is symbolically inherited in our own conscience. Every being is Arjun standing in the middle of two armies, in 'No man's land' caught within the bondages of the rival forces which disintegrate his being, his instincts at the end are governed by humanity, to perceive enemy as a being of flesh and bone rather than succumbing to hypocritical ideology of nationalism.

Andha Yug as a title is relevant in contemporary times, depicting how a modern man is blind in the race of gross materialistic comforts, insatiable lust for power and is in the frenzies of territorial expansion. *Andha Yug* is an age where there exist several shades of human follies which further culminates the question of survival of the entire humanity. Set in the evening of the eighteenth day of the *Mahabharata*, when both sides, victors Pandavas and the vanquished Kauravas, are fraught with self-doubt about the relevance of war and are frustrated and shocked with its devastating powers. They realize that the consequences of the war travelled beyond their control, when Ashwatthama refused to listen to any logic and released the *brahmastra* that would destroy all irrespective of which side they stood for, the right or wrong. It is then they begin to introspect if the war was inevitable, if both sides erred, if everyone had a role in inviting the volcanic eruption of violence.

War is rampant with ways of misconduct, deceit, duplicity that even the Krishna of the *Mahabharata* does not exist in the absolute, God-like form but as a more humanly cherished figure, so much harm the war has caused on the virtues and morality that even Krishna was at times chastised and at other times cursed, at times if he was loved or worshipped, on the other he was abandoned and hailed to have a single-minded conviction. Virtues have become a utilitarian service which can be called in to help when we are in trouble and forgotten about at most of the times. The ramparts are in ruins, the city is burning and both the Kurukshetra and the Front is covered with corpses and vultures.

The ordinary foot soldiers of both the sides are cynical about those who control the affairs of state. They are more concerned about their immediate survival than about questions of law or virtue. Dynasties change and fall, but the never-quenching, tormenting fire still gnaws everyone in its clasp.

> That day the world descended into the Age of darkness which has no end and repeats itself, over and over again, every moment the Darkness grows deeper and deeper. The age of Darkness has seeped into our very souls and there is a blind doubt and shameful sense of defeat. (Bharati, *Epilogue*)

Work Cited

Remarque, Erich. *All Quiet on the Western Front*. Trans. Brian Murdoch. London: Vintage, 1994.

Bharati, Dharamvir. *Andha Yug*. Trans. Alok Bhalla. New Delhi: Oxford University Press, 2005.

Reorchestration of Cultural Consciousness in John Barth's *Giles Goat-Boy*

SOUMY SYAMCHAND
Res. Sch., Annamalai University
A. SELVARAJ
Annamalai University

Disenchanted and distorted by the sway of technology, man loses his individuality, and subsequently, identity. John Barth, the representative postmodern American writer, depicts the plight of contemporary humanity caught in, rather than sustained by, a culture that celebrates the carnivalesque of technology, dissolution of identity, and death rather than humanity and life. The theme of mythical revival is as old as the Socratic pronouncement: "Know thyself." Yet, from Oedipus Rex to Jacob Horner, this has been the undercurrent that enables the literary/ critical text afloat, whirl or sink. However, the search for the self/ identity has basically remained a monolithic phenomenon and narcissistic in its framework from the traditionalists and even to the modernists. Although the modernists were bewildered by the divided/ disintegrated self, they still held firm conviction that the self can be integrated through an inner sense of unity. The postmodernists who ruled out even this meagre contingency given to self, "identity," "self" and "ego" in a postmodern slippery ground have multi-dimensions. Ego, in its original sense, is seen as a mask. The self is not seen as a separate entity that the individual can afford to be narcissistic about anymore. The boundary of the self is made visible only in contra-distinction with the other. Semantically speaking, the self is not to be found in itself but in the other. The conventional markers of these aspects are blurred. Hence "identity" has become a fluid concept.

The American society is multi-cultured, and there is no special culture to hang on. We can see an aching of past culture in most of the postmodern writings. This paper reflects on the Barthesque dissemination of identity in terms of anonymity, pathology, control systems, fragmented society, and deflated myths. The society is fragmented, the people ache for their identity, and their nihilistic mentality leads them to nothingness. Most of the inhabitants of America are migrants, and they have no special culture to hang on to. In the multicultural society, they lost their tradition and faced the after-effects like suicide, abortion, lack of love etc. Conflict between many of their inherited beliefs or rather tradition leads them to absurdity. This explicates that beliefs, customs, and ethics are relative to the individual within his own social context. Right and wrong are culture-specific; what is considered moral in one society may be considered immoral in another, and since no universal standard of morality exists, no one has the right to judge another society's customs.

Barth's fourth novel *Giles Goat-Boy* marked a significant stage in Barth's career in which the range and direction of his interests changed. As with most issues concerning Barth, however, our understanding of this change is necessarily paradoxical. Cultures are worthy in their own right and of equal value. In his, *Giles Goat-Boy*, Barth is quite articulate about the philosophical problem he is intrigued with so as to make it the theme of the investigation by his protagonist-narrator, George Giles. The question George Giles asks is what Albert Camus called "the fundamental question of philosophy" in *The Myth of Sisyphus*, that is, the meaning of life in the world where man has lost his faith in God. The novel itself is presumably an attempt of the narrator to explain the process and the outcome of his Inquiry about the question of meaning of life.

Despite the gloomy subject matter, Giles's recollection is full of comic renditions of life. Critics have praised and detailed his comic and satiric use of the mono-myth of the hero as well as the many allegorical levels of *Giles Goat-Boy*. But many have also found the book tedious and boring, largely because the mythic pattern, and thus the book's basic plot, are essentially known from the beginning; though Barth makes a mystery of some elements such as the identity of George's father, the course of his life is never in doubt. Of interest, given the book's long and often repetitive nature, are the details that make Barth's story unique in the evolution of his themes and technique as these are woven into new designs on this basic structural framework. Barth has said that he intended *Giles Goat-Boy* to be more than just a satire of the hero myth, that he aimed to "escalate the satire into something larger, darker, and more compassionate" (Meras 22). Beneath its satirical and mythical surface, Giles is indeed "something larger, darker, and more compassionate." And beneath the admittedly tedious working out of the rather formulaic plot lies a new and exciting step in the evolution of Barth's concept of love.

In this novel, Barth again addresses the connection between identity and intimacy, the difference between animal love and human love, the conflict between one's calling and one's personal relationships, and, as always, the desire for wholeness that may be gained through love. The myth of the hero, as it turns out, provides more than just a mere framework for Barth's concerns; its traditional themes of the hero's quest for self-identity and wholeness mirror Barth's own. As Joseph Campbell observes, "The passage of the mythological hero may be over ground, incidentally; fundamentally it is inward" (29). In his archetypal journey, George struggles over much the same psychological terrain as Barth's previous protagonists, though taking a slightly different course, travelling toward a different destination.

The multiple frames surrounding the story of George's life and the questionable identity of its author make *Giles Goat-Boy* a more complex work than Barth's earlier fiction. In discussing Giles, it makes most sense to begin at the centre with the story of George, the Ag-Hill goat boy, and then work outward through the frames that not only surround the central tale but impinge upon it. Not surprisingly, George is cut from the same fictional cloth as the protagonists who have preceded him, especially the young Eben Cooke of *The Sot-Weed Factor*, but his story takes on a new appearance with the addition of two major metaphors: the translation of "universe" into "university," turning the world into a college campus, and the correspondence between the term for young goats and human children, making the young George a "kid" who spends his childhood as a goat. George's early identity and his gradual transformation from goat into man emphasize one of Barth's recurrent themes—the task of becoming fully human, accepting and coping with the things that set men apart from animals: the power of imagination, the awareness of death, and the ability to love singularly and passionately.

Though *Giles Goat-Boy*, like Barth's other novels, has its share of sexual couplings of all sorts, it emphasizes, as previous works have done, the difference between sex and love, and its bawdy surface covers a deeper investigation of intimate relationships. Sex is easily understood by the goatish George; it is love and marriage that puzzle him. George's story, while chronicling his archetypal heroic adventures, also charts his emotional growth, observable in two converging lines of inquiry: his effort to understand the relationships (all of them problematic) of the couples he meets, and his attempt to comprehend his own involvement with Anastasia and their feelings for one another. George's path crosses that of three other couples, all examples of failed or perverted relationships that could serve as case histories for the course on "Problems of Modern Marriage" (457). As George tells Peter Greene, "I hadn't appreciated how curious marriage is, and I'm interested to learn now whether it's that way generally. The only other married folks I've met are Mr. and Mrs. Stoker and a Dr. Sear and his wife and their attitudes seemed a little different from yours and Mrs. Greene's, at least to me" (290). Anastasia explains that her marriage to Maurice Stoker "was strictly a business deal" (187) which turn out to be a sadomasochistic relationship; she becomes "the mistress of Stoker's every whim and craving which, he hinted darkly, were as infinite in number as they were bestial in character" (188). Child's development occurs through his relationship with his love object, i.e., his mother, so George's growth takes place through his relationship with his primary love object Anastasia, who often functions much like a mother. Not only does she represent the "Universal Mother" (Campbell 113) in the book's mythological schema, but in her personal relationship with George she performs the functions of the good mother, one of the most important being the "mirroring" she provides.

The descent into WESCAC is, in many ways, a return to the original symbiotic unity with the mother, embodied physically in the womb-like "belly" of the computer and the "oneness" George enjoys with Anastasia. But as her name, Greek for "resurrection" or rebirth, reveals, she also provides the means of George's psychological birth as an individual in his own right. Martin S. Bergmann points out that "love revives emotions that once belonged to the symbiotic phase," and observes: "The separation-individuation phase has its contribution to make to the capacity for love. It is during this phase that the child first learns to be separate in the presence of the mother" (33). George's relationship with Anastasia graphically illustrates this development. He is never more aware of himself as a separate person than he is with Anastasia when the "final shadow" disappears and he sees himself as an individual loved by her. Only then, secure in the knowledge of himself, does he experience, in mature love, the feelings once active in the symbiotic phase. George is more successful than any of Barth's previous protagonists in satisfactorily resolving the issues of separation and individuation.

Typically for Barth, the emphasis falls on the men George, Sear, and Greene, and as might be expected, they share certain similarities. Each exemplifies the theme of *Giles Goat-Boy*, the journey from self-ignorance to self-awareness, the growth of a fragmented psyche into a whole and integrated self. And each is thus characterized by one of the major metaphors of taboo—the difference between "seeing" with the eye and "seeing" with the understanding. Finally, each illustrates the connection between knowledge of one's self and the ability to love and be loved. The presentation of Kennard Sear and, even more obviously, of Peter Greene, reflects the paradox that lies at the heart of *Giles Goat-Boy* thematically and technically. Both men are obvious parodies, stereotypical characters, and yet beneath this seeming shallowness, they convey deep emotional truths. We are thus simultaneously confronted by the "unreality" of the exaggerated parodies while forced to acknowledge the validity of the feelings they express. Not only are the parodic elements necessary as part of the satire of *Giles Goat-Boy*, but they also provide some distance from the emotions of marital failure and middle-age distress which find their first, controlled, expression in this book; in *Lost in the Funhouse* and *Chimera* they will be dealt with more directly.

Peter Greene, as his name implies (green, naive), is a parody of American innocence, whose childhood satirizes everyone from Huck Finn to the young Abe Lincoln (271). His resulting condition combines the feelings and philosophies of Todd Andrews, Jake Horner, and Eben Cooke. He experiences "periods of impotence," and a "sense of futility" and takes to "rocking in a chair" (282). No longer believing in the Founder (God), he realizes that "Nothing in the University mattered in the long run" and attempts suicide by taking an overdose of sleeping pills. When he wakes the next morning, he, like Todd Andrews after his failed suicide attempt, he turned one of Barth's famous corners:

> Nothing had changed: there was still no Founder, nor any sense in the University . . . there was still no more reason, ultimately, to heed the summons of his bladder and children than not to. Yet all these truths had a different feel now; he kissed Mrs. Greene and left the bed, still utterly uncertain how his life was to be managed and heedless of its course, but with a new indifference to this indifference. (283)

Giles Goat-Boy emphasizes the fragmentation of the psyche that all humans experience, attested to by the myths of all ages. While Eben attains wholeness only through a symbiotic reunion with his twin, George achieves a greater wholeness of the self, enabling him to unite with Anastasia in a mature sexual relationship. Since identity is one of George's major problems, it seems appropriate that his enemy, the anti-Giles Harold Bray, is a creature (perhaps not human) in the nature of Henry Burlingame, though more sinister. While Bray, too, has "several roles attributed to him under different names and appearances" (370), he literally wears masks that peel off only to reveal another mask. Like the onion that has no core beneath its layers, so Bray seemingly has no real self beneath his many masks.

Even the larger elements of *Giles Goat-Boy*, such as the boundary dispute between East Campus and West Campus, reveal the intra-psychic conflict that underlies the story. The two computers EASCAC and WESCAC; "from a special point of view it might be argued . . . were brothers or even the hemispheres of a single brain" (95). And the philosophies they espouse pit the selflessness of the Student Unionists against the selfishness of the Information lists. As aspects of "a single brain" they not only illustrate the need for wholeness through the reintegration of polarities but illuminate the relationship between self and other. Selflessness, in the extreme, leads to loss of the self through merger with others, while selfishness may result in individual isolation. The question of personal wholeness and the issues of separation and fusion are thus intimately connected and never more so than in the relationship of George and Anastasia.

Feeling as though "my mind must crack," George finally explains, "I gave myself up utterly to that which bound, possessed, and bored me. I let go, I let all go; relief went through me like a purge" (709). The same acceptance is required of "this thing from Sub-Departments of Sentimental Literature, this love" (671), and of the mind-boggling prospect of being loved. As Menelaus will make even clearer when his situation with Helen repeats that of George with Anastasia, it is impossible to know why one is loved; one can only let go of the need for rational answers and accept the irrationality and absurdity of love, as of life. Having attained a sense of personal identity and wholeness, George goes farther than any previous protagonist in his development. Yet his emotional life, too, leaves much to be desired. After his moment of illumination in the belly of WESCAC, the symbolic Axis Mundi or World Navel of the mythological cycle, life is never again so bright.

Works Cited

Barth, John. *Giles Goat-Boy*. Greenwich, Conn.: Fawcett, 1966.

Campbell, Joseph. *The Hero with a Thousand Faces*. 3rd ed.1949; rpt. Princeton, N. J.: Princeton University Press, 1973.

Bergmann, Martin S. "Psychoanalytic Observations on the Capacity to Love," *Separation-Individuation*: *Essays in Honor of Margaret S. Mahler*, ed. John B. McDevitt, M.D. and Calvin F. Settlage, M.D. New York: International Universities Press, 1971.

Meras, Phyllis. "John Barth: A Truffle No Longer," *New York Times*, 7 August 1966, 22.

Devastating Effects of Synthetic Pesticides: Rachel Carson's *Silent Spring*

HEMA VARSHA K.
Res. Sch., Presidency College, Chennai

People have been fighting environmental injustice for a long time, and many of them were women. Karen L. Kilcup and Robert K. Musil introduced to the nineteenth and twentieth century women who combined scientific, cultural and political insight with literary talent to engage both the emotions and the consciences of everyday American readers. Rachel Carson, Betty Friedan and Jane Jacobs opened vast new possibilities for social transformation by writing about widespread attacks on nature, women and the poor.

Rachel Louisa Carson (27 May 1907-14 April 1964) was an American marine biologist, author and conservationist, who grew up in the rural river town of Springdale, Pennsylvania. Her writings are credited with advancing the global environmental movement. Her mother bequeathed to her a life-long love of nature and the living world that Rachel expressed first as a writer and later as a student of marine biology. Carson early developed a deep interest in the natural world. During the 1950s, she conducted research on the effects of pesticides on the food chain and published her findings in her most influential work, *Silent Spring* (1962), which condemned the indiscriminate use of pesticides, especially DDT. The book led to a presidential commission that largely endorsed her findings, and helped shaped a growing environmental consciousness.

Carson was worried that chemicals such as DDT had been rushed into large-scale usage before anyone had researched on its environmental effects. She sought to bring the world's attention to evidence researchers were accumulating showing that pesticides were killing many more creatures than just their intended targets. These chemicals were being sprayed routinely over large tracts of land in America and elsewhere.

Chemical companies sought to discredit her as a communist or hysterical woman. Many pulled their ads from the CBS Reports TV special on April 3, 1963, entitled *Silent Spring* of Rachel Carson. Still, roughly 15 million viewers tuned in, and that, combined with President John F. Kennedy's Science Advisory Committee Report, which validated Carson's research, made pesticides a major public issue. Carson received medals from the National Audubon Society and the American Geographical Society, and induction into the American Academy of Arts and Letters.

Carson was attacked by the chemical industry and some people in the government as an alarmist, but she courageously spoke out to remind readers that they are the vulnerable part of the natural world subject to the same damage as the rest of the ecosystem. Testifying before Congress in 1963, Carson called for new policies to protect human health and the environment. Rachel Carson died in 1964 after a long battle against breast cancer, her witness for the beauty and integrity of life continues to inspire new generations to protect the living world and all its creatures. She was the founder of the environment movement.

The main theme of *Silent Spring* is the deconstruction of delicate balance of nature by the whole-sale use of insecticides. Carson carefully explains what the balance of nature is. She describes the balance of the nature of the soil, of the earth's water, of the organisms on the earth. In *Silent Spring,* Carson assembled information on chemicals used in aerial sprayings, in industrial settings, and on food to characterize the impacts of these agents in ecological terms rather than simply portraying the effectiveness of the chemical solutions. Carson built her case on science. She did extensive research, citing dozens of scientific reports, conducting interviews with leading experts, and reviewing materials across disciplines. The minor theme of the novel is the alternatives to chemical poisons for controlling insects. At every point at which Carson describes the destructiveness of chemical poisons on the ecosystem, she also informs the reader of alternative methods of accomplishing the same ends. The alternative methods work with nature's already existing balance and help it along. They are cheaper and safer than insecticides.

Carson had become interested in the danger of pesticides while still associated with the Fish and Wildlife Service. Her concern was accelerated with the introduction of DDT in 1945. Although she had left the service to work on *Silent Spring*, her marine studies while there had provided with early documentation on the effects of DDT on marine life.

Carson had long been aware of the dangers of chemical pesticides but was also aware of the controversy within the agricultural community, which needed such pesticides to increase crop production. She had long hoped someone else would publish an exposé on DDT but realized finally that only she had the background as well as the economic freedom to do it. She made the decision to produce *Silent Spring* after years of research across the United States and Europe with the help of Shirley Briggs, a former Fish and Wildlife Service artist who had become editor of an Audubon Naturalist. Clarence Cottam, another former Fish and Wildlife Service employee, also provided Carson with support and documentation on DDT.

Silent Spring begins with the tale of a fictitious town epitomizing middle-America. The town becomes blighted: sheep and cattle sicken and die; people fall ill in ways doctors have not seen before; there are unexplained fatalities; the birdlife disappears; the bees disappear and the orchards bear no fruit; vegetation withers; and the rivers are lifeless--the fish have all died. There is no malign outside influence to blame for the disaster; the people have caused it themselves with their use of chemicals. The poisons they forced upon the environment have come back to attack them.

Carson describes a community in which all the elements of the natural world, including humans, work together and are able to enjoy the sound of birds and the growth of spring. Suddenly chemical poisons are introduced and the spring is silenced. There are no more birds to sing in the spring. This sad world is what Carson is concerned in *Silent Spring*.

Nature and literature are always linked together, and eco-criticism deals with the literature that focuses on "green" and only the true facts. In this non-fiction, Carson describes the relationship between literature and the physical environment. Though she was attacked by the government and the chemical industry as an alarmist, she courageously spoke out to remind that they are a vulnerable part of the natural world subject to the same damage as the rest of the eco-system.

Eco-criticism is the study of the relationship between literature and physical environment. Eco-criticism takes an earth-centred approach to literary studies. Human culture is connected to the physical world, affecting it and being affected by it. Eco-criticism takes as its subject the interconnections between nature and culture, specifically the culture artefacts to language and literature. As a critical stance, it has one foot in literature and the other on land; as a theoretical discourse, it negotiates between the human and the nonhuman. Barry Commoner states his first law of ecology, "Everything is connected to everything else," and this also means that literature does not float above the material world in some aesthetic, rather, plays a part in an immensely complex global system, in which energy, matter and ideas interact.

Cheryll Glotfelty, one of the pioneers in the field, defined eco-criticism as the study of the relationship between literature and the physical environment. Eco-criticism is still in its infancy. It deals with ecology, environment, surrounding, biotic or abiotic etc. It cannot be defined so easily. The term "eco-criticism" was coined in 1978 by William Rueckert in his essay "Literature and Ecology: An Experiment in Eco-criticism."

In 1991 MLA organized a special session entitled "Eco-criticism; The Greening of Literary Studies." In 1992 a new Association for the Study of Literature and Environment (ASLE) was formed. Its mission was to promote the exchange of ideas and information pertaining to literature that considers the relationship between human beings and the natural world and to encourage new nature writing, traditional and innovative scholarly approaches to environmental literature, and interdisciplinary environmental research. ASLE's membership topped 750 by 1995 and the group held its first conference, in Fort Collins, Colorado. In 1993, Patrick Murphy established a new journal, *ISLE: Interdisciplinary Studies in Literature and Environment*. Thus by 1993, ecological literary study had emerged as a recognizable critical school. The formerly disconnected scholars joined forces with younger scholars and graduate students to become a strong interest group with aspirations to change the profession.

Cheryll Burgees Glotfelty is Associate Professor of Literature and Environment in the University of Nevada at Reno, United States of America. She has written several essays on eco-criticism, Women Writers and Western American Literature. She co-edited with Harold Fromm, *The Eco-Criticism Reader: Landmarks in Literary Ecology* (University of Georgia Press, 1996), that helped green the field of literary studies. Her most intense interest is the connection between literature and the environment. She promulgated the concept of "eco-criticism." She produced an anthology of eco-critical essays. She has become the first American professor of literature and environment. She is the co-founder and past president of the ASLE.

The earliest American settlers had two conflicting viewpoints on nature. Native Americans or the Indigenous people viewed the natural world as part of themselves. They believed that both are part of a continuous cycle of giving and receiving. To them, nature is perfect and does not need to be modified. The contrasting view is that of the early American settlers up to present day Americans. Most Americans saw nature as something to be perfected, considering themselves outside nature. Most felt that it was their right to rule the land and to modify it for humans. "There was once a town in the heart of America where all life seemed to live in harmony with its surroundings" (21)

The literary piece deals with a city in USA, where people thrived in harmony. Thriving farms surrounded the town and every spring there were fruits and flowers in abundance. When people travelled to the area, they enjoyed the variety of plants. This was a land that was beautiful in spring.

Carson describes a community, in which all the living elements of the natural world, including humans, work together, and are able to enjoy the sound of birds, and the growth of the spring. Man and nature lived together and believed that both are part of continuous cycle of giving and receiving. They maintained a mutual relationship and during that period the spring season seems to be very pleasant and adorable. The countryside was famous for the abundance and variety of its bird life. "Along the roads, laurel, viburnum and alder, great ferns and wildflowers delighted the traveller's eye through much of the year." (21)

Man enjoyed the roads while travelling to the countryside. The roads were filled with great ferns and wildflowers. Suddenly, something happened and everything started to die. No one could account for the strange kind of symptoms people, birds, and animals started displaying. Many creatures died. Sometimes children would be playing and suddenly they would be stricken with something and die only a few hours later. People wondered what had happened to the birds. The birds that remained were often so sickly that they could not fly. Chickens still laid eggs, but the eggs did not hatch. The apple trees put out blossoms, but no bees came to pollinate them. The countryside that once looked so pretty now looked dry and withered. People noticed a fine, white dust had settled all over the leaves and in the gutters of their houses. The problem with this land had not come from witchcraft, but from the people themselves. "No witchcraft, no enemy action had silenced the rebirth of new life in this stricken world. The people had done it themselves." (22)

Chemical poisons were introduced by man and were used for pest control in farms and other places. Many chemical poisons were introduced by man and used for different purposes. Without recognizing the devils of his own creation, he created everything. Man started to move away from nature, instead of living in harmony with nature, humans had chosen to take up arms against it.

The most alarming of man's assault upon nature was the contamination of air, earth, rivers and sea with dangerous and even lethal materials. The use of chemical poisons for the insect control, such as DDT and Arsenic, affected the process of the world. These chemicals had the power to kill every insect, the "good" and the "bad." It was not only the insects, but also other birds, animals, plants, human beings which were affected. "For the first time in the history of the world, every human being is now subjected to contact with dangerous chemicals, from the moment of conception until death." (31)

DDT (dichloro-diphenyl-trichloro-ethane), "a war hero," a "magic" was created by humans and sprayed all over the fields of America. It was the most powerful pesticide the world had ever known, exposing nature's vulnerability. Unlike most pesticides, whose effectiveness was limited to destroying one or two types of insecticides, DDT was capable of killing hundreds of different kinds at once. DDT was originally envisioned as a miracle chemical that would improve the quality of human lives at relatively low risk to people. It killed mosquitoes and lice, later it was permitted by American army scientists to be used as pest control.

Nature has its own insect control and other alternative processes. But man does not realize the use of natural aids for insecticides. He tries to control nature with his own creation. Many scientists have started to discover new insecticides for pest control. These chemicals were used in different fields and both man and nature were affected. This new tide of chemicals represented a drastic change in public and environmental health. Instead of infectious diseases like smallpox or cholera, man now concentrates on those potentially harmful things in our environment like radiation and chemicals--that have been introduced into the world by man. They have the power to render the world uninhabitable, silent and birdless.

Nature is filled with everything; it has thc solution for its own problem. No other external power like humans should have control over it. Many alternatives have been in use which are dangerous to nature. They mostly involve widespread contamination of the natural world that spurs "a chain of poisoning and death." "Man is more dependent on these wild pollinators than he usually realizes." (77)

Some insects are essential for agriculture. Insects like honeybees and wild bees depend heavily on weeds such as goldenrod, mustard and dandelions for pollen that serves as the food for their young. The spraying of DDT and arsenic affected the roadside vegetation and also the agricultural farms. The use of chemical pesticides increased considerably after World War II, ecological damage was noticeable by the late 1940s. Pesticides come in two common types: insecticides, which kill insects, and herbicides, which kill weeds. DDT is a synthetic man-made chemical insecticide. DDT was successfully used during World War II to control malaria and other diseases carried by insects.

After the war, it was adopted widely to kill insects damaging farm crops and other insect pests.

For the first time in history, human beings are exposed to dangerous chemicals from the moment they are conceived. These substances are found everywhere: in organisms in remote lakes, earthworms burrowing in the soil, and humans all over the world. Their production began during WWII and has grown rapidly ever since. New pesticides are incredibly potent, Carson warns, with the ability to affect important processes in the body. "The Second World War marked a turning away from inorganic chemicals as pesticides into the wonder world of the carbon molecule, a few of the old materials persist." (32)

Arsenic is chief among the older, inorganic pesticides. It is still the basic ingredient in a variety of weed and insect killers. It is a highly toxic mineral occurring widely in the association with the ores of various metals, in the sea, and in spring water. It is naturally occurring in small amounts, and highly toxic a favourite poison since the time of the Borgians, an infamous dynasty during the Italian Renaissance.

Arsenic contamination kills many species and has carcinogenic (cancer-causing) effects on humans. Arsenic-contaminated environments have also caused sickness and death among horses, cows, goats, pigs, deer, fish, and bees. But still with all these records, arsenic sprays and dusts are widely used. Farmers using arsenic dusts have been afflicted with chronic-arsenic poisoning. Livestock have been poisoned because of the spray on weed killers containing arsenic.

DDT is often thought of as harmless because it was used in powder form to combat lice during WWII. It was first synthesized by a German chemist in 1874. At first it was believed that it is harmless. There are no immediate ill effects. DDT in powder form is not absorbed through the skin, in liquid form it is much more toxic and can accumulate in the body over time. If the DDT is swallowed, it is absorbed through the digestive system and also through the lungs. They enter the body and are stored largely in organs rich in fatty substances, such as adrenals, testes, or thyroid. Large amounts are stored in liver, kidney and parts of intestines. "The poison may also be passed on from mother to offspring. Insecticide residues have been recovered from human milk in samples tested by Food and Drug Administration scientists." (37)

The chemical is transmitted through the food chain, and even from mother to child. If a crop of alfalfa is dusted with DDT, and chickens are fed with infected alfalfa, their eggs have been shown to contain DDT afterwards. The same mechanism of transference has been found to function in human mothers who transmit DDT through the placenta during pregnancy or in their breast milk. "Dr. Lehman has described chlordane as 'one of the most toxic of insecticides'--anyone handling it could be poisoned." (38)

Chlordane is another chlorinated hydrocarbon which has all the unpleasant attributes of DDT. It easily penetrates through the skin. Like other chlorinated hydro carbons, its deposits build up in the body and also pass on to next generation. On the other hand death may strike quickly.

Dieldrin, named after a German chemist, Diels, is about five times as toxic as DDT when it is swallowed. When it is absorbed through the skin in solution, it is forty times toxic than DDT. Dieldrin is one of the most used insecticides today. Despite the appalling destruction of wildlife it is used worldwide. "Dieldrin is one of the most used insecticides today, despite the appalling destruction of wildlife that has followed its use. As tested on quail and pheasants, it has proved to be about forty or fifty times as toxic as DDT." (39)

Like dieldrin, alderin is extremely toxic. It makes changes in the process of liver and kidneys. Endrin is the most toxic pesticide of all. For birds, it is 300 times more toxic than DDT. Endrin has killed enormous numbers of fish, cattle and other animals. One of the most tragic cases of endrin was of carelessness; efforts had been made to take precautions apparently considered adequate. American parents in Venezuela used some chemicals to kill the cockroaches. After a few days a spray containing endrin was used. The baby and the small dog were taken away before the spraying. The floor was washed and the baby and dog returned home. After an hour the dog vomited, went into convulsions, and died. At 10 p.m. on the same day the baby also vomited, went into convulsions and lost consciousness. The child became little more than a vegetable unable to see or hear, the drastic happening was only due to the chemical sprayed to destroy the insects. "The organic phosphorous insecticides act on the living organism in a peculiar way. They have the ability to destroy enzymes--enzymes that perform necessary functions in the body." (42)

The second major group of insecticides includes the alkyl or organic phosphates, which are among the most poisonous chemicals in the world. Organic phosphates, the second group of pesticides, have their origin in German labs, where they were discovered by a chemist named Gerhard Schrader and then weaponized during WWII as nerve gas. They attack the nervous system, destroying enzymes that are vital to the proper transmission of impulses from nerve. Without this enzyme, an excess of transmitters builds up, causing convulsions and death. Parathion is one of the most widely used organic phosphates. It is one of the most powerful and dangerous chemicals. Honey bees become more agitated while in contact with parathion. A chemist thinking to learn the harmful effects by direct possible means swallowed a minute amount. Paralysis followed so quickly that he could not reach the antidotes he had prepared, and he died. It is now said to be a favourite instrument of suicide in Finland. Yet some 7,000,000 pounds of parathion are now applied to fields and orchards of the United States, by aeroplane, by hand-sprayed, motorized blowers and dusters. The chemical sprayed in the fields of California farms alone could provide a lethal dose for five to ten times the whole world's population.

Herbicides, poisons that target plants, are also toxic, and the myth that they are no threat to animal life is false. Many have been banned in England and Australia, although no such restrictions exist in the United States. Dinitro, penta, and amitrol are examples of herbicides with hidden, cancer-causing effects that can sometimes be transferred down the germ line, meaning that their effects carry on from one generation to another. "Aerial spraying has widened and its volume has increased so that it has become what a British ecologist recently called 'an amazing rain of death' upon the surface of the earth." (142)

Dr. Otis Poitevint, a veterinarian, saw many sick farm animals, including a calf that was exposed via his mother's milk. The ant poison was sprayed all over the place to kill ants but other birds and animals suffered a lot. Cattle, goats, horses, chickens, and birds and other wild life began to suffer fatal disease of the nervous system. These animals were affected due to the contaminated food or water. Other animals were not affected. This condition could be seen in the areas treated for fire ants. "Over increasingly large areas of the United States, spring now comes unheralded by the return of the birds, and the early mornings are strangely silent where once they were filled with the beauty of bird song." (100)

Chemical poisons are used in every corner of the house. From shelf paper treated with insecticides to solutions rubbed directly onto the skin to paint and varnish which comes pre-treated with poisons, the common household is becoming a dangerous area. No one is telling people of the dangers. The U.S. Department of Agriculture even encourages the use of insecticides in the home, urging people to spray their clothing with oil solutions of DDT, dieldrin, chlordane and other moth killers. Finally, in 1960, the Florida State Board of Health forbade the use of pesticides in residential areas without a permit. They took this action only after a number of deaths by parathion happened. Dieldrin has long delayed effects including memory loss, insomnia and nightmares. Lindane has long-lasting effects on the central nervous system.

Spraying is not the solution to the problems of insects in forests. Natural parasitism can be used a method of finding the insect that is the enemy of the targeted insect and introducing them into the forest. Micro-organisms can be introduced which will serve as diseases to the target insects and thus kill them off naturally. There are many alternative approaches to pest control that pose no risk to both the environment and humans. These alternatives are called "biotic controls," and are divided into three specific methods.

The first method would use chemicals found within the insects themselves to repel the insects or trap them. Instead of using a poisonous and harmful chemical, it uses the insect itself to control the pest population. This is an environmentally acceptable means of pest control. The second method would require sterilizing male insects and introducing them into the pest population. This would gradually reduce the volume of the pest population. The third uses both natural bacteria and insect predators to kill off pests. Allowing insects to kill each other off does not harm the environment the way pesticides do. "In my opinion too much is taken for granted. We do not know whether all weeds in crops are harmful or whether some of them are useful," says Dr. Briejer. Charles Darwin published a book *The Formation of Vegetable Mould through the Action of Worms, with Observations on Their Habits.* He gave the world its first understanding of the fundamental role that earthworms play as geological agents for the transport of the soil. This shows the importance of the earthworms for both plants and the soil.

The problem of keeping budworm control is another problem. Budworm caterpillars are considered serious pests because of the amount of damage they can do to plant life by feeding. Instead of spraying toxic chemicals to kill budworms, the method of natural parasitism is an alternative way. It was first proposed by Erasmus Darwin in 1800. Since all insects have "many natural enemies," including microbes and other insects, E. Darwin proposed controlling insects by using other insects to kill the pest insect. In Canada the pest control becomes very challenging; so they found the natural predators from North America and introduced them into Canada. The shrews could eat large number of cocoons, this would result in natural pest control. A shrew can eat up to 800 cocoons per day, reducing the amount of cocoons in an area by 75 to 98 percent.

The awareness began only after some mass destruction in both human and non-humans. Man should recognize the things happening around him. He should maintain good relationship with nature and conserve it. Chemicals that are used not only affect the targeted insects but harm both humans and non-humans. It is that rather than being distinct from nature and able to disregard it, humans are part of nature, and nature is part of humanity. Everything is interconnected, and the biological systems work as cycles, that humanity is very much part of it. Man does not always know the consequences of their actions.

The novel *Silent Spring* is the documentation of Carson's research on the effects of pesticides on the environment. *Silent Spring* began with a 'Fable for Tomorrow'--a fiction followed by a true story using a composite of examples drawn from many real communities where the use of DDT had caused damage to wild life, birds, bees, agricultural animals, domestic pets and even humans. People started using the pesticides, without knowing the full extent of their potential harm to the whole biota. These chemical pesticides deposits over the plants, animals, birds, human beings, and other living and non-living organisms on earth. It started affecting both human and non-human with mass destruction. The spring, suddenly became silent without any bird song and the trees failed to bloom with attractive colours. The spring always gives some delightful pleasure to everyone, but here in this novel it is portrayed as "silent" spring to show the impact of the environment.

This critical condition of the environment first seen in America was later found in all places around the world. Man and nature are always interdependent; humans could not survive without the help of nature, but his war against nature destroyed it. The disturbance in nature results in disturbing man. If man started war against nature, then nature would take up war against man, this could be seen in the novel as 'Nature fights back.' The chemicals were created by human beings to fight nature. Chemicals like DDT and arsenic are very powerful and started destroying the environment. Many scientists have been fighting hard to find an alternate way. Some of them have given suggestion for reducing weeds and insects by using natural methods.

To save the environment and the earth, everyone must follow the natural method instead of using chemicals. *Silent Spring* by Rachel Carson portrays the harmful effects of manmade chemicals and creates awareness among the readers to protect the environment for the future generations. The future generations should have some purified air, water, and soil to lead a happy life.

Works Cited

Carson, Rachel. *Silent Spring*. Boston, London: Penguin, 1962.

Allex, "Devastating Effects of Synthetic Pesticides in Rachel Carson's *Silent Spring*." 123Helpme.com.

Glotfeltty, Cheryll and Harold Fromm, ed. "The Eco-Criticism Reader." *Landmarks in Literary Ecology*. Athens, GA: University of Georgia Press.

Goodboy, Andy, and Kate Pigby, ed. "Ecocritical Theory; New European Approaches." Charlottesville: Univ. of Virginia Press, 2011.

Mishra, Alok. "Ecocriticism Theory in Literature: Introduction and Analysis." *Alok-mishra.net.*Biharsharif

Book Reviews

Gopichand, *Asamardhuni Jeeayatra*, Trans. with Introduction by D.S. Rao, *The Bungler: A Journey through Life.* New Delhi: Srishti, 2003. 168 pp.
Gopichand, *Merupula Marakalu*, Trans. with an Afterword, *Usha Rani: A Tale of Sense and Sensibility.* New Delhi: LiFi, 2013. 183pp.

Dr. D.S. Rao who retired from service in 1991 as the Secretary of the Kendriya Sahitya Akademi is a versatile writer, translator, and literary critic who edited the well-known journal *Indian Literature* for a number of years. His translations of Gopichand's novels *The Bungler: A Journey through Life* and *Usha Rani: A Tale of Sense and Sensibility* bring the distinguished originals enshrined in the memory of Telugu-speaking people to a new life in English. His Introduction to *The Bungler* is impressive. It traces briefly the history of the rise of the Telugu novel and attempts to establish a definitiveness about the works to be considered in the context. Incidentally it gives authentic information about the first novels in the various Indian languages, leading women writers gaining popularity from the serial publication of their novels, and prominent men writers who withstood possible usurpation of their creative space by a display of their unique creativity. Akkiraju Ramapathi Rao's view that Narahari Gopalakrishnamma Chetty's *Rangaraja Charitra* (1872), described by the author as "naveena prabandham," should be considered the first novel cannot probably be easily contested. Maybe a lot more research ought to take place on the issue. *Rangaraja Charitra* was dedicated to Lord Mayo and the Fort St. George Gazette described it as "apparently the first attempt ever made . . . at novel writing in Telugu prose." It is a novel set in the fifteenth century and traces the customs and rituals prevalent at that time. In respect of Kandukuri Veeresalingam's *Rajasekhara Charitra*, serialized in 1878, the appellation "novel" was conferred by Kasibhatta Brahmayya Sastri. Rather than go by the usage, "nava" and so on, one feels that the Telugu critics need to arrive at the form and characteristics of the novel as they conceive them in a mode of critique that compares with the Western idea of the novel.

The Telugu novel absorbed features from Henry Fielding and the novel of manners, Richardson and the epistolary mode as also "the psychological sentence of the feminine gender," the cultural and rhetorical elements of the picaresque tradition of narrative which originated in Spain and led to the development of realism. Rao cites how Chilakamarti Lakshminarasimham was hailed as the Andhra Scott. An authentic history of the rise of the Telugu novel, like Ian Watt's *The Rise of the Novel*, is the need of the hour. If the influence of the English, or more broadly the European tradition, was due to Anglomania on the one hand and the "treason of the clerks" on the other, the influence exerted by the Russian novel was due to cultural and ideological reasons. In the nineteenth century England, novel in serialized form became popular and sociologically this was attributed to the rise of the middle class. Such sociological studies too seem to be relevant in the context of Telugu literature and the various ideological and artistic turns it has taken.

D.S. Rao's depiction of Gopichand's portrayal of the contrarieties of human personality through the portrait of Sitarama Rao, his tracing of the anti-hero tradition in the novel and its features of existentialism which sees the in-itself and for-itself relationship as creating an intrinsically uncertain self-identity, his observation that there is strain of magic realism in the novel, and his final remark on a careful reflection on the novel that it follows the Zola strain of naturalism and offers a subversion of existentialism and Marxism make for a comprehensive interpretation of the novel's themes and the strains of thought it has absorbed. When one reads Gopichand, not in the original but through the English lens D.S. Rao has provided, one is not really convinced about the Zola strain nor about the magic realism component, though one notices the evocation of the element of fantasy in the novel. D.S. Rao has clinched the issue of the Gorki heritage in his characteristic call-a-spade-a-spade approach. The sidelights he has given in the context on literary borrowings and comparative studies that highlight speculations about cross-cultural influences settle the issue once for all. Sheridan's Mrs. Malaprop rightly said that caparisons were odorous, implying comparisons were odious. Jung speaks about archetypes based upon Plato's Ideas and Schopenhauer's prototypes as an a priori "psychic orderedness" and these primordial archetypes, images and topoi form the hinterland from which the writer seeps in, though he is bound by the time and space coordinates.

Then D.S. Rao at the end refers to the translator having to serve two masters: the author in the source language and the reader in the target language. Between these two, there is what is called the language of the least compromise, English, which conjures up a world and culture its own in relation to which the poet R. Parthasarathy expresses his predicament in the words, "my tongue in English chains." In addition it must be borne in mind that translation does not reproduce the original but renders it. There is a lot of theoretical discussion on this into which we need not go at this stage except saying that translation is an "after life" of the original which gives wider audience to the original. We should also bear in mind the fact as Homi Bhabha put it that flitting across cultures as we do "we are translated men" launching on translation as an academic activity.

D.S. Rao has taken up two challenging novels for translation. If *The Bungler* interests the reader as a bold experiment in technique, *Usha Rani* raises expectations of the feminist mode but transcends it by tracing a journey from hedonism to asceticism. The disbelief in the rise to asceticism of Usha Rani raises an interesting debate in the novel which reminds one of Shaw's *Mrs. Warren's Profession* where Shaw, combining moral seriousness and light comedy, deconstructs the woman with a past and the underlying conservative ideology and blames both female depravity and male licentiousness while outlining the role of circumstance and other factors.

D.S. Rao's justification of why he chose to name the novel after its heroine instead of finding semantic equivalents for *Merupula Marakalu* shows his concern for dynamic equivalence on the one hand and his obeisance to a mentor figure Krishna Kripalani and his mode of approach. "Merupula Marakalu" seems an instance of the use of a mixed metaphor. There is an implied reader, a presumed addressee, in every writer's mind as part of the structure inscribed in the narrative. Balachandra Rajan's *Paradise Lost and the Seventeenth Century Reader* keeps the seventeenth century reader and his universe of knowledge and mythology at the centre in an understanding of the poem *Paradise Lost*, for the poem was primarily addressed to him and so his perspective on the poem had a validity all its own. The poststructuralists have gone a step further to posit the reader in the narrative. D.S. Rao has made a philosophically weighty statement at the end of his "Afterword" that allegorizing literary characters, finding their equivalents among us, is a high tribute to the creativity of the writer. Coleridge said that in reading *Hamlet* we discover an otherness in ourselves.

Both *The Bungler* and *Usha Rani* read well in English translation. The obstacles that the translator encounters have been meticulously analyzed and the reasons for the subtitles explained. Stylistically speaking, D.S. Rao's two translations capture the rhythms of the originals so that the flavour of the Telugu narratives or their raciness is not lost in translation. One is reminded of a profound utterance by Arundhati Roy on *The Ministry of Utmost Happiness* that it is a novel written in English but imagined in several languages because in a sense every language is infused with many languages. The translation of a literary text is not so much a transaction between two languages, or an act of linguistic "substitution" as Catford had put it, but something of a complex negotiation between two cultures. The unit of translation is not the word or the page but the whole language and culture in which the text is situated. Described as "the Cultural Turn in Translation Studies" (see *Translation, History and Culture*, 1990, by Susan Bassnett and Andre Lefevere), it has revitalized the discipline. D.S. Rao's translation bears this in mind.

Hyderabad **C.R. VISWESWARA RAO**

Saikat Majumdar, *College: Pathways of Possibility*, Bloomsbury, 116 pp.

With the onset of the second term of Modi government at the centre, education is deemed to be an important area where a number of changes are expected to be made. The budget for education is bound to go up several notches. However, in this kind of scenario, the quality of education being imparted and the possibilities available do deserve our attention.

The present book *College: Pathways of Possibility* by Saikat Majumdar, a university professor, is a forceful plea for moulding the present 'artscience' education in India along a more liberal line and making it truly liberal arts education. Liberal Arts, as a stream of learning, started in the US as a reaction to the overmuch stress on technical education. In India, it was first tried at Flame Institute (now a university) Pune and later it entered other universities--Symbiosis, O.P. Jindal Global, Ashoka, etc. The pace has been slow, and for understandable reasons.

Drawing heavily upon educationists Howard Gardner and John Dewey, this 100-odd page book, nevertheless, is a forceful articulation of Majumdar's ideas based upon his own life experiences and insights that he formed as a student and as a teacher. Add to this, his standing as a novelist and you can appreciate the narrative style that amalgamates personal anecdotes making the book a fascinating work.

Majumdar's recapitulation of his student days in Calcutta and the kind of literary study that the students normally did at that time is the springboard for visualizing this book. He was also disturbed by the news of the suicide by Alankar Jain who was preparing to crack engineering entrance exam at Kota--a place well known for preparing students to that end. The writer's intent to underline the uninspiring, taxing and unimaginative courses that have come down to us since Macaulay's days becomes clear from the title of the first chapter "The Clerical."

The writer's reminder that the European universities including the British were much different from the ones the colonizers set up in India primarily to "conduct examinations and award degrees" is a clichéd one, but the rejoinder that these did not even offer courses in science and were by no means meant to foster liberal thinking which would have fostered in the native people the tendency to question authority is indeed needed in these times.

Regarding the "unnatural exclusion of the basic sciences from the liberal arts family," he believes that it has "turned the latter impoverished, the humanities parochial, and science bereft of the big questions it is meant to ask." To buttress his point, Majumdar explores the domain of human intelligence and discusses the various intelligences like linguistic, logical-mathematical, musical, interpersonal, body-kinaesthetic, etc. as outlined by the American psychologist Gardner, whose theory has been opposed as not being based on empirical research even though a lot of pedagogical material based on his theory is available. (Incidentally, Gardner has read Majumdar's book and his comment on it forms one of the blurbs adorning the book.)

That said, one cannot disagree with Majumdar when he says, "Learning a subject is not merely about covering a canon in detail or taking in a lot of information; it is also assuming the very mode of thought that defines and distinguishes that particular discipline." The understanding of the epistemic form of disciplines and to hone the skills through this understanding is indeed desirable. And the best way, according to the author, to achieve this goal is to compare and contrast a discipline with another. Herein comes the importance of contra-discipline study where the student takes up in addition to his chosen area of specialization, another subject to realize the distinction that while literature is interested in the particular, social sciences take up the general. Ditto for the human and the natural or the private and the social. Together, these impart a holistic education.

Other aspects discussed by the author include the general education component of undergraduate courses, the psychological aversion for the core courses against the fascination for the elective ones, the artificiality of separation of teaching and research institutions, which he calls a colonial legacy, and the need to articulate research findings in simple ways so as to make an undergraduate understand it. In this context, he aptly quotes the leading physicist Richard Feynman's response, who, finding it difficult to prepare a lecture for an undergraduate class on a tedious concept, remarked, "That means we really don't understand it." That shows indeed the true concern for scholarship and the urgency to transmit it to the young people.

As the liberal arts study gains momentum in India, several questions pertaining to the availability and the finance for a large number of qualified faculty members, employability (not every employer understands the worth of a liberal arts graduate yet) stare us in the face. The new draft education policy on higher education has devoted a lot of attention to liberal arts programme though in its own way. We have to wait and watch how the final policy implementation takes place.

The narrative of Majumdar's book is made lively with several anecdotes based on the writer's personal experiences as a student and a teacher at several renowned institutions, even if it might appear to be meandering at times. The novelist's art comes to the fore wherever the factual sags. Overall, it is a book worth-reading and mulling over.

O.P. Jindal Global University, Sonipat JAGDISH BATRA